NBA
ROOKIE EXPERIENCE

WHAT'S IT REALLY LIKE TO PLAY IN THE NBA? FIND OUT FROM THE NEW STARS THEMSELVES!

Mike Monroe

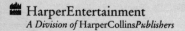
HarperEntertainment
A Division of HarperCollins*Publishers*

To the ladies I love:
Cathy, Melanie and Mary

 HarperEntertainment
A Division of HarperCollins*Publishers*

10 East 53rd Street, New York, NY 10022–5299

Third stanza from the poem "Midway" by Naomi Long Madgett appears on pages 124-5. © copyright 1957. Reprinted by permisson of the author.

ISBN 0–06–105935–8

First paperback printing: November 1998

Printed in the United States of America

Visit HarperPaperbacks on the World Wide Web at:
http://www.harpercollins.com

❖ 10 9 8 7 6 5 4 3 2 1

Contents

Introduction

The simulation could take place in a conventional setting with the traditional trappings of the sport—a gym with a shiny orange goal and a varnished hardwood floor. It also could occur on a gritty asphalt playground, concrete driveway, or even in a barnyard with dirt flattened and hardened from years of pounding sneakers and basketballs. Or maybe it is in the sanctity of a kid's room with a jutted-out hanger jammed between the top of the door and the door frame and with a rolled-up pair of socks serving as the basketball.

The fantasy is accompanied with a play-by-play. *Michael Jordan has the ball at the top of the key. He fakes to his left, loses the defender, takes two quick steps to the right, pulls up, shoots a 17-foot jumper and . . . HE SCORES!*

The dream is shared by every child who has ever picked up a ball, or acceptable facsimile, and tried to toss it through anything serving as a hoop. The National Basketball Association. Basketball at its highest level, where the rewards are measured in millions of dollars and those who reach it can become international icons.

There was a time when the path to the NBA was clearly defined. Kids were introduced to the game in grade school, they learned the fundamentals in junior high and high school, then refined their skills and established their reputations in college. NBA scouts critiqued their play and made recommendations to general managers who would pick players in the NBA draft, and the best would move on to stardom.

The goal became reality.

But the process has dramatically changed in the final decade of the twentieth century. Today, an NBA first-round draft pick may be a teenager who has graduated from high school, or a star player from Europe, Africa, or Australia. The singular path to the pro game has divided into many divergent avenues. The backgrounds are diverse and varied, and that means the adjust-ments are, too.

No matter how they arrived at the highest level of play in the world, however, all first-year NBA players share one trait: They are rookies, all fac-ing the greatest adjustments of their lives.

NBA Rookie Experience is the story of the adjust-ment to NBA life from the perspective of six dis-parate first-year players: from the fortuitous expe-rience of Tim Duncan, the very first selection in the first round of the 1997 Draft, with a team con-tending for an NBA championship; to that of Bobby Jackson, a late first-round pick whose mis-fortune it was to land on a team that would find itself running to escape the misery of the worst record in NBA history. From the wrenching adjustment of teenager Tracy McGrady to a com-pletely new level of play and expectation, in a dif-ferent country and on a team that underwent cat-aclysmic change at midseason; to the strange odyssey of Chris Anstey, at one time one of the top junior tennis players in tennis-crazy Australia, a player who already had played basketball professionally in the Australian pro league for two years. From the experience of laid-back Keith Van Horn, yanked out of the nurturing sanctuary of easy-paced Salt Lake City to the hubbub of the greater New York City area, burdened with unfair comparisons to one of the greatest players ever, Larry Bird; to the unusual experience of point guard Jacque Vaughn, the penultimate pick in the first round, who expected to go to Salt Lake City and apprentice under one of the league's great point guards, minus the great expectations often unfairly placed on first-round picks, only to be thrust into prominence when Dream Teamer John Stockton suffered the first serious injury of his career during training camp.

Each experience was different, yet all six players shared a common bond: the *NBA Rookie Experience.*

one
The Luck of the Lottery

When Tim Duncan was a junior at Wake Forest in 1996, there was only one mystery involving his position in the NBA Draft. Would he be the first pick in 1996 or in 1997? Duncan had a decision to make. Would he pursue the Holy Grail of college basketball, the NCAA championship, and stay in college all four years? Or would he leave after only three years and accept the millions of dollars that are guaranteed to the premier college player in the country?

When Duncan announced in late April 1996, that he was eschewing the draft to remain in school, he became the toast of college basketball and a supreme disappointment to the 13 non-playoff teams that would participate in the 1996 NBA Draft Lottery. One of them would have had the good fortune to select him with the first pick in the 1996 Draft. Duncan, a 7-footer with rare skill, grace, and basketball acumen, immediately would have transformed a very bad NBA team into a team with hope.

Duncan had just been named Defensive Player of the Year by the National Association of Basketball Coaches; was a consensus All-American player; had led the prestigious Atlantic Coast Conference in rebounds and blocked shots; and finished second in scoring and field-goal percentage. NBA scouts were unanimous in the opinion that he was destined for greatness.

Instead, with Duncan unavailable, the team that won the draft lottery in 1996, the

Philadelphia 76ers, selected a player nearly a foot shorter, point guard Allen Iverson. Iverson, both a mercurial player and personality, would become the 1996–97 NBA Rookie of the Year, but he hardly would turn around the 76ers. Indeed, Philadelphia found itself back in the draft lottery in 1997, with the second pick in the first round.

The team with the second pick was not going to get Tim Duncan.

Who, then, would win the right to pick an impact player as capable as any top draft choice in the final decade of the century? Would it be another team whose record was so dreadful the previous season, a roster so devoid of talent as to make an immediate turnaround unlikely, even with adding a player like Duncan? Would it be one of the marginally bad teams at the bottom of the lottery list, defying the odds intentionally stacked against such vagaries of fortune? Or would it perhaps be a team, the San Antonio

Spurs, whose very presence in the studios of NBA Entertainment, in Secaucus, New Jersey, on draft lottery day was purely an aberration of misfortune?

San Antonio had been one of the best teams in the NBA's Western Conference from the day, in 1989, that David Robinson had been allowed to turn in his uniform as a lieutenant, junior grade, in the United States Navy, for the one bearing the Spurs' logo. The Spurs had won the draft lottery in 1987 after going 28–54 and had made Robinson the first pick in the draft, despite the fact that he was obligated, as a graduate of the United States Naval Academy, to serve five years in the U.S. Navy. The Spurs knew at the time there was a strong likelihood Robinson, too tall to serve as a naval line officer aboard ship, would be allowed to shorten his active duty to two years, maybe less.

They chose him, and when he was released from active duty in 1989 and joined the

team, the Spurs went from 21 victories to
56. Robinson was the unanimous choice as
Rookie of the Year, and the Spurs became a
perennial force in the Western Conference.
From 1989 through the 1995–96 season
they won no fewer than 47 games, and in
1994–95 they won an NBA-best 62 games,
advanced to the Western Conference Finals,
and Robinson was selected as the Most
Valuable Player in the league.

In 1996–97, however, misfortune struck
the Spurs, and the results were disastrous.
Robinson suffered from a lower back strain
and missed the first 18 games. He returned
for six games in December, then broke the
fifth metatarsal bone on his left foot. He
missed the remainder of the season.

Robinson's wasn't the only injury to
befall the Spurs. Veteran Chuck Person, a
long-distance shooter of such extraordinary
skill that he was referred to as "The
Rifleman," missed the entire season with

back problems. Starting forward Sean Elliott played in only 39 games because of chronic tendinitis in his right quadriceps. Forward Charles Smith appeared in only 19 games because of arthritis in his right knee.

In short, the Spurs went from one of the best teams in the league to one of the worst. They finished with a record of 20–62, third-worst in the NBA, behind only the Vancouver Grizzlies, 14–68, and the Boston Celtics, 15–67.

On draft lottery day, the Spurs were assigned 157 of 1,001 chances in the 13-team drawing to determine the first three picks in the draft. Gregg Popovich, San Antonio's coach and general manager, didn't believe there was any way that his team could be so lucky as to land the first pick. That, he believed, would go to Boston, which had 264 chances to win the number-one pick. Vancouver had 250 chances, but under terms of its 1995 expansion agreement, the

Grizzlies could not get a number-one pick until 1999.

Duncan watched the lottery proceedings in St. Croix, Virgin Islands, where he grew up, but he did not think about playing for the Spurs. He watched as the order of the draft was announced, beginning with the thirteenth pick. When the envelope revealing the team with the third pick in the draft was opened, the Celtics' logo appeared. At that point Duncan knew he was not going to Boston.

"I sat up in the chair when Boston came up early," said Duncan, who then knew he was going to go to San Antonio or Philadelphia. "I wasn't really rooting for any team to get me. It didn't matter. But I got up and ran around the room a little bit when San Antonio got me."

Spurs officials and fans were doing the same thing in front of their TV sets in San Antonio. Suddenly, the Spurs had become

the luckiest team in the NBA, but Duncan
was the truly lucky one. The downside of
being the first selection in the draft usually
is that the player is sentenced to play for a
bad team, one that has earned the right to
select first through the ineptitude of the
previous season. The first pick is thus burdened with the expectation that he will lead
his team out of the NBA's doldrums to the
promised land of playoff success.

Such would not be the case, though, for
Duncan. Instead, the best big man to come
out of the college ranks since Shaquille
O'Neal enjoyed the prospect of playing
alongside Robinson, a former MVP and
member of three Olympic teams, including
two of the NBA-dominated Dream Teams,
and the most athletic 7-footer in the game.

Duncan would have the luxury of playing
both power forward and center, not to men-
tion the knowledge that the pressure for the
Spurs' success would continue to reside

squarely on the broad shoulders of Robinson, the man known as "The Admiral."

"I think I was really blessed," Duncan told the *San Antonio Express-News* in a post-draft interview. "We have an opportunity to win a lot of games our first year, and that's different from most number-one picks [who have] to go in and rebuild a team."

Duncan was totally unconcerned that he might not be the center of attention, which is usually the case for the first player taken in the draft.

"Not at all," he said. "I think it will really help me a lot. It will give me a chance to grow with not as much pressure on me. At the same time, I can help the team in my own way. I think I can do a job of relieving some stress off David. It's good turning around and having somebody by your side who can really help you out defensively, on the glass. To have that strain on one person is a real big deal."

Not all the pressure would melt away with Duncan's good fortune, though. Spurs players and fans immediately saw the team rising back to championship caliber.

"We are back," said point guard Avery Johnson, one of the team's captains, after watching the lottery proceedings. "That's all I've got to say. That will be our new motto."

Fans were even more excited. Longtime Spurs supporter Roy Garrett told the *San Antonio Express-News*, "This can put us in a championship mode. We can trade for a couple of good players or keep Duncan. Either way, we'll be a contender."

And there was this from Peter Holt, Chairman of the Spurs' ownership group: "I thought we could easily win 50 games with the team we had, if it was healthy. If Tim Duncan is all that we believe he is, you've got to believe he puts us in a league of our own."

A league of their own? Had Holt not

heard of a fellow in Chicago named Michael Jordan? A team called the Bulls that had won five championships in the 1990s? Did the owner of the Spurs really believe they had become the best in basketball by getting Duncan? Maybe. Maybe not. But there was no way Popovich would consider trading Duncan before the draft, unless, of course, guys like Magic Johnson and Larry Bird somehow found the fountain of youth and returned to the league. It would have taken players of that stature to pry Duncan out of San Antonio.

"I guess if you put a package together of Larry, Michael, and Magic, then you could make a trade," Popovich said. "But that's not going to happen."

Popovich discovered when he returned to San Antonio how excited the populace was at the prospect of getting Duncan. "It's basically a fiesta town," he said. "Everyone is always ready to party and relax. People were already excited about our injured players coming back, and then when Tim Duncan fell in our laps, by an unbelievable stroke of good fortune, they were very excited."

With the city and team already gaga over him, the Spurs surprised absolutely nobody when they made Duncan the first pick of the 1997 NBA Draft, which was held at Charlotte Coliseum, not far from where Duncan played his four years of college ball.

Duncan was one of 15 players, all of them expected to be among the early selections, the NBA invited to the draft. When draft day finally arrived, Duncan met it with confidence, knowing the Spurs would make him the first pick. His only real concern was that he might trip and fall on his way to the podium after being announced as the number-one pick.

That faint uncertainty disappeared when

it was time for the Spurs to actually exercise their right to make that first selection. When NBA Commissioner David Stern announced that the clock was ticking on the five minutes San Antonio was allotted, Duncan's heart began to pound, faster with each minute that passed.

"I began to entertain a series of second thoughts," Duncan said, "and the Spurs didn't help by taking all of their allotted time. After one minute passed, my heart began to lightly patter. After two, that patter became a flutter; at three, a thump; at four, a palpitation; and at five, just as I was on the brink of full-blown cardiac arrest, the commissioner rescued me from oblivion with this announcement: 'With the first pick in the 1997 NBA Draft, the San Antonio Spurs select Tim Duncan, from Wake Forest.'"

The pressure gone, Duncan spent the next half hour doing more interviews for print reporters and TV and radio stations.

Finally, though, he could contemplate the rest of his life, now to be experienced in a new environment. What would San Antonio be like?

He found out when the Spurs flew him to the Alamo city the next day to meet the local press and to appear at a rally on the steps of the Alamo. Duncan was overwhelmed when 6,000 San Antonians jammed into Alamo Plaza to cheer his arrival in their city. The pep rally included the Spurs' mascot (the Coyote, one of the NBA's first costumed animal mascots and a celebrity in its own right in the city), the Spurs dance team (the Silver Dancers) and the team's pep band.

"This is incredible," Duncan told the crowd. "I can't believe you all came out like this. It's great down here. I hope to see you all at a game. I don't know what else to say."

Duncan signed a contract in early July, and then Popovich approached him with a suggestion that he feared Duncan might find a little insulting. Popovich wanted to sell Duncan on the idea of participating in the team's summer camp for rookies and free agents and playing in the Rocky Mountain Revue, a 12-team competition in Salt Lake City for rookies and free agents. Most of the players had little chance of making an NBA roster. They were trying to impress scouts and possibly earn a spot as an 11th or 12th man on the team. A player of Duncan's stature seldom participated, although there was one major exception. In 1989, Robinson had played in a similar summer league before his first season with the Spurs.

Popovich began talking to Duncan about playing, but before he had gotten too far down his list of reasons, Duncan interrupted him and said, "Pop, is it important that I go there?"

"I really think it will help you," Popovich answered back, somewhat startled.

"I'm there," Duncan replied.

It was important to Duncan to get off to a good start in his pro career, and he had welcomed the chance to come to San Antonio and get on the strength and conditioning program of team specialist Mike Brungardt. Going to play in Salt Lake City was no big deal.

When Duncan arrived in Utah, he discovered more about the expectations that would be placed on him as a heralded rookie. With his arrival came a flood of interview requests from media representatives ranging from a columnist from the *Provo Daily Herald* to David Aldridge, the respected NBA correspondent from ESPN.

Duncan just wanted to go about the business of learning to become a pro. He said he had no specific goals for the Rocky Mountain Revue. But everyone who attended a game at the Delta Center, including Utah Jazz star Karl Malone, who was on hand almost every day, knew one thing:

Duncan had better earn tournament Most Valuable Player honors, or someone would have to answer why.

Duncan did not disappoint. To be fair, the competition hardly pressed him. There is a particularly acute shortage of truly talented big men, so Duncan figured to have his way at the Revue, and he did. He was the Revue's leading scorer and rebounder and, yes, the tournament's Most Valuable Player.

The Revue completed, Duncan didn't have to do anything else, officially, under Spurs' supervision until the start of training camp. But he reported to San Antonio in the first week of September so he could participate in informal pickup games with some of his new teammates. He arrived with his business manager, Marc Scott, who is a close friend and former Wake Forest teammate, and the two hurried off to close a deal on the home Duncan had purchased. He wanted all such distractions behind him before camp opened on October 1.

"I'm trying to be a good player," Duncan said. "I don't want to be just another body. The way you do that is you go in and you start working."

Duncan had been overwhelmed by the friendly reception he had gotten from the people of San Antonio, who had amazed him by turning out by the thousands at that Alamo Plaza rally the day after the draft.

"The pressure I feel to perform is rooted, at least partially, in a desire to return the tremendous goodwill extended to me by the people of San Antonio. I have, in a sense, been adopted by the city. Everywhere I go, I am met with kindness and encouragement.

"But underlying the outstretched arms and supportive words is a base of lofty expectations that I do not want to disappoint."

When October 1 arrived, he was more than ready.

two
The (Bad) Luck of the Draw

It wouldn't be fair to say Bobby Jackson was an uninvited guest at the 1997 NBA Draft, even though the league did not fly him to Charlotte and put him up in a hotel, all expenses paid, as it did for the top 15 prospective draftees.

It didn't have to. Jackson grew up in Salisbury, North Carolina, only 45 miles from Charlotte, a local hero despite the perception he didn't quite measure up to the next level of basketball. And since he was already in the neighborhood, Jackson decided to drop in at the Charlotte Coliseum.

"The NBA gave me a whole bunch of tickets because they knew I had a lot of family and friends in the area," Jackson said. "I was a little mad because I thought [the NBA] should have invited me, but I still thank them for giving me all those tickets."

Jackson was accustomed to proving himself. After he led his Salisbury High School team to the North Carolina prep championship game in 1992, he could not immediately play at a major college because of academic deficiencies.

Instead, he went off to Scottsbluff, Nebraska, to play at Western Nebraska Community College, precisely 1,784 miles and approximately 100 light-years from Salisbury.

"Nothing but cornfields," Jackson said, hardly wistful.

He didn't exactly get off to a good start. In his first practice at Western Nebraska, Jackson tore a knee ligament. But after two difficult years he finally was ready for major college. He chose the University of Minnesota, where he eventually became Big Ten Player of the Year after a stellar 1996–97 season. He was not really a point guard, but at 6–1, he was considered too small to be an NBA shooting guard. He would have to prove himself again, this time to the NBA.

He went to the Desert Classic in Phoenix, a tournament designed to help NBA teams identify pro prospects, and was named to the All-Tournament Team. He wanted to play in the Chicago Pre-Draft Camp in June, but a sore hamstring dictated otherwise. Jackson then went on the pre-draft audition tour, working out for and being interviewed by a dozen teams.

As draft day approached, Jackson returned home to Salisbury, where he showed up at Livingstone College to take several dozen youngsters to Pizza Hut for lunch. The college had conducted a "Bobby Jackson Basketball Camp," at which he had committed himself to appear and participate. But his busy pre-draft schedule made that impossible, so Jackson spent the day before the draft treating all the campers to pizza.

Draft day arrived and Jackson, wearing a new suit, sat in the stands with his family and closest friends and advisers. While Jackson would have liked to be invited by the NBA, league officials knew there was a chance he would not be selected in the first round.

So Jackson sat in the stands with the people who cared most about him, including his mother, Sarah, who had shaped his work ethic and his approach to life.

"To just go down there and be supported by all those people was great," Jackson said, "but it was kind of scary because I thought I would go between 10 and 17."

He didn't. And with each name

announced, Jackson's heart sank deeper into a pit of fear and depression.

"After the 17th guy was called, I told my mom, 'I'm ready to go,'" Jackson remembered. "I hadn't worked out for anybody after 17. Those teams didn't know anything about me besides watching me at Minnesota."

His head spinning, his heart sinking, Jackson took solace in a gentle hug from his mother. He swallowed hard and listened intently for his name to be called next, and never considered there might be a trade brewing between one of the teams yet to pick and another team—one more desperate for an infusion of immediate talent.

Finally, with only seven picks remaining in the first round, Jackson heard NBA Commissioner David Stern intone the words he had been desperate to hear all night: "With the 23rd pick in the draft, the Seattle SuperSonics select Bobby Jackson, from the University of Minnesota."

A huge cheer erupted from the packed Coliseum house, thrilled another North Carolina native was off to the NBA. Jackson jumped up from his seat into his mother's arms. He turned and hugged most of his closest friends as he made his way from the stands to the Coliseum floor. He mounted the podium and shook hands with Stern, sporting the SuperSonics cap he had been handed on his way to meet the commissioner.

Photos were taken, Stern and Jackson holding a handshake for nearly a minute as the photographers snapped. Jackson walked down the stairs and was escorted to the interview area. His heart was racing. Jackson opened his post-draft press conference by saying how happy he was to be going to a great team like the SuperSonics, where he could learn behind a great player like Gary Payton.

Then Jackson received the first surprise of his NBA career. A reporter from Denver told him he was not going to Seattle. The

SuperSonics had traded his draft rights to the Denver Nuggets, a team that had finished with the fourth-worst record in the NBA the previous season, and a team that had not invited him for a workout.

"I hadn't heard nothing about any trades," he said. "I couldn't believe it. I was like, 'For real?'"

It was real, all right, and it was hard to digest.

"I was already happy I had gone in the first round," Jackson said. "It would have been nice to play in Seattle, a sure playoff team of championship caliber. But I remember thinking I wouldn't get to learn as much in Seattle as I would in Denver. I probably would have played 10, 12, 15 minutes a game for Seattle. When you've got a guy like Gary Payton, you need him out there."

Jackson celebrated his first-round selection with family and close friends, and finally, long after midnight, tried to get to sleep in his Charlotte hotel room. But he couldn't.

"All I could think was that all the hard work I had gone through had paid off," Jackson said. "That was one of my goals, just to get to the NBA. I was thinking, 'I've made it, and I can't stop now. I've got to be the best player I can be.'

"I thought about how I was going to be able to take care of my family . . . a thousand things running through my head. I was still in shock. There's such a small percentage of players who ever get to play at this level, and I just felt the Lord had blessed me to get to play in the NBA."

It would be many months before Jackson would begin to wonder if the blessing was more like a curse. On draft night his trade to the Nuggets seemed like incredible good fortune. Not only would he be going to a team without an established point guard, but he would be a mere three-hour drive from Wheatland, Wyoming, where his two children, Breann and Kendrick, lived with their mother, Georgann O'Neill. Jackson had met O'Neill at Western Nebraska, not all that far from Scottsbluff. A two-year relationship didn't work out, and the couple never married. But Jackson had provided for the two children, even while he was in college, and had insisted on being a part of the children's lives from the day each was born.

Now he was going to Denver, where he could hop in a car and be in Wheatland in less than three hours under ideal conditions.

"That's one reason I was so happy about being traded to Denver," Jackson said, "and that's why I want to stay here my whole career. I'm closer to them [his children] and get to see them a lot more than if I were in Seattle. That's one reason I felt fortunate to be here.

"I want to be able to go up there and see them and teach them the things that my mom taught me. I want them to be around me and show them the things that my dad didn't show me."

When Jackson was just two years old, his father had abandoned him, his twin sister, Barbara Ann, and his mother. Jackson had made a promise to himself, very early in life, that he would never abandon a child of his own.

The next day Jackson flew to Denver to meet the press and the Nuggets brass. Immediately, he found out doubts other NBA teams had about his ability to play point guard in the NBA weren't shared by then-Nuggets coach Bill Hanzlik and then-Vice President of Basketball Operations Allan Bristow.

"They had traded for me, and they had expectations for me," Jackson recalled. "A lot of people didn't think I could play the point guard position at this level. That was the word that had gone around. But they had a lot of confidence in me, to bring me to Denver and welcome me with open arms. I knew they didn't have a starting point guard, and I had a good chance of coming in and playing a lot of minutes to help this team out.

"I think it was good luck for me, just to be drafted in the first round, though I thought it should have been higher. That's just me. If you can't have confidence in yourself, you can't expect other people to have confidence in you. But I always knew I could play at this level. I'd been through so much, my five years of college, and just to be here, playing with the best players in the game, that meant a lot."

Hanzlik and Bristow told Jackson how important it would be for him to immerse himself immediately in a summer conditioning and development program. That program included playing with a Nuggets team at the Rocky Mountain Revue, a tournament where NBA teams could get a look at rookies and free agents hoping to fulfill their dreams.

"I wanted to come up here and show them the dedication they showed to me by trading for me," Jackson said. "I just wanted to come up here and get familiar with the area, get settled into my own place and start out fresh and right."

The fact that he could spend every weekend with Breann and Kendrick was a major bonus.

"In the summertime I had to work out every day," Jackson said, "but weekends, I got to see the kids and bring them to Denver with me. It worked out real good."

At the Rocky Mountain Revue, Jackson erased any doubts the Nuggets and other NBA personnel may have had about his ability to play the point.

"I went over there to Utah and played great defense and ran the show," Jackson said, "but I tried to do too much. I made a lot of mistakes, a lot of turnovers. I learned a lot from turning the ball over so much. I learned I have to make the easy play rather than trying to make the hard play, the great one. I get caught doing that sometimes. But I'm learning to distribute the ball more, and that's why I like it here. I wouldn't have learned in Seattle because I wouldn't have played that much."

The first Sunday of the tournament, a scheduled off day for the Nuggets team, Jackson was startled when his hotel room phone rang shortly before 8:00 A.M. It was Hanzlik calling, and he told Jackson to meet him in the lobby in ten minutes. Hurry, Hanzlik said, this is important.

Jackson dressed quickly in his sweats and went to the lobby, where Hanzlik, Bristow and the other Nuggets draft picks—Tony Battie, Danny Fortson and Eric Washington—were waiting.

"We were wondering what he was doing," Jackson said of Hanzlik. "We didn't have practice that day, but he woke us up and walked us down to an athletic club next to the Delta Center. We were like, 'What are we doing here?' and he just said, 'You'll see.'

"And Coach took us downstairs, and there was Karl Malone teaching a cycling class, a spinning class. It was real intense. He had those people in there sweating. Coach did that just to let us know how hard we have to work. Karl was the MVP of the league, and he's not letting up. Coach did that to teach us what we needed to do to stay in the league a long time. Karl told us we had to take care of our bodies, and you have to work at it to condition yourself. I was surprised that so soon after the NBA Finals, he was back in the gym. He wants it so bad; his dedication is so tremendous. That says a lot for a man like that to talk to us like that. He wants to win the NBA championship, and he's always striving for that goal."

For Jackson the brief meeting with the reigning NBA MVP was the highlight of the summer. When October arrived, he was ready for training camp. But before camp, the Nuggets made a personnel move that would dramatically affect Jackson's rookie season. Worried that their best player, power forward Antonio McDyess, would bolt from the team the next summer when he became a free agent, the Nuggets traded McDyess to the Phoenix Suns for three future first-round draft picks and two future second-round draft picks.

Suddenly, the team's immediate prospects dimmed, but Jackson plowed ahead. He was intent to prove the Nuggets made the right choice when they obtained his rights.

"I just knew I had to work on my skills to get better as a player, so I wouldn't let the coaches down," he said. "I had to play my game, like I did in college and in the Rocky Mountain Revue. They had a lot of confidence in me then, and had a lot of confidence in me now. I have a lot of confidence in myself, too. I can compete with the best of them."

Less than 10 days into training camp, it was evident Jackson was the best point guard in camp. Hanzlik pulled him aside a few days before the team's first exhibition game and told him he had won the starting job.

"I didn't call nobody up or anything," Jackson said. "I was just determined in my mind I was going to go out and do my job, play hard and prove to everybody I could play the position. I expected to win it [the starting job]. With the way that I play and the confidence I have, I had to expect it. I'm going to compete with the best of them, regardless of whether it's Tim Hardaway or Gary Payton. I'm going to play with confidence."

Three days later, Jackson was introduced

to a big crowd at the San Diego Sports Arena as the Nuggets' starter in the exhibition opener against the Los Angeles Lakers, one of the preseason favorites to win the NBA's Western Conference title.

"I was nervous," Jackson said. "I'd never been put in a situation like that. The Rocky Mountain Revue was nothing like that. Those were guys trying to make NBA teams. The competition wasn't as good as it was going to be against other NBA teams. I was anxious to get it under way. I think I did okay, even though we got blown out. We were young and hadn't jelled. But I was just happy to be out there with Shaq [Shaquille O'Neal] and Kobe [Bryant] and Eddie Jones and Nick Van Exel. I was in awe, but I had to put that aside and just go out and play."

The exhibition season was a blur, and the Nuggets won three of eight games. Finally, the regular season arrived. Opening night was at Denver's McNichols Sports Arena, against the San Antonio Spurs and their prized rookie, Tim Duncan, the first player taken on the night Jackson had to sweat through the first 22 picks.

"I was just into myself that evening," Jackson said. "I had worked so hard just to get here, and now they were saying my name . . . 'At guard, from Minnesota, Bobby Jackson.' I couldn't even believe it. I just wanted to play hard and try to get a win and do the best I could do. I know Tim had been hyped up by everybody to be Rookie of the Year since the night of the draft. So I just wanted to play hard and show everybody what I could do."

What Jackson did was score 27 points, as he sparked a late Denver rally that fell short in a 107–96 loss.

"I was disappointed I had only one assist," Jackson said of his first regular-season game in the NBA, "but you learn from every game you play. You have to learn from each game."

Before the game started, Vicki Michaelis, who covers the Nuggets for the *Denver Post*, had learned the Boston Celtics had offered to trade Chauncey Billups, the third pick in the draft and a Denver native who was a local legend, to the Nuggets for Jackson. Straight up.

The Nuggets had said, "No thanks," and Michaelis discreetly told Jackson after the game about the trade that hadn't happened.

"I remember Vicki telling me the Celtics had offered Chauncey Billups for me and the Nuggets had turned it down," Jackson said. "That made me feel great. I know Chauncey is a great player, and he grew up here in Denver and had a lot of fans here, so for the Nuggets to choose me over him had to mean a lot to me.

"I knew what I had to do not to let them

down: Go out and prepare myself every day
and get better as a player."

Little did Jackson know on that night, the
last night of October, nothing would get
better for the Nuggets.

three
Touting Van Horn

Consensus opinion that had Tim Duncan as the certain first pick in the 1997 NBA Draft had a huge impact on the future of Keith Van Horn. Teams knew there was no way they could pry the number-one pick out of San Antonio, so the epicenter of trade talk was in Philadelphia, where the 76ers had the second pick in the draft.

Van Horn's talent made scouts drool. At almost 6–11, he was tall enough to position himself inside and battle for his share of rebounds. But he also had excellent quickness for a big man, and, most important, he had tremendous shooting range. The three-point shot was almost effortless for him.

Some scouts, in fact, believed that Van Horn was only infinitesimally less talented than Duncan, with a chance to be every bit as good a pro player.

Having gone to college at the University of Utah in Salt Lake City, where he was a local basketball icon in one of the smallest cities to have an NBA team, Van Horn believed he would be most comfortable in the pros in an atmosphere not much different than what he had encountered in college. The Jazz, of course, had no shot at drafting him, having compiled the second-best record in the NBA the previous season, when they won the Western Conference title and pushed the Chicago Bulls to six games before succumbing in the 1997 NBA Finals. Still, Van Horn made it clear before the draft that he preferred to stay out West, but there was a problem. Of the four teams with picks immediately behind San Antonio's, two were from the East—Philadelphia and Boston—and two were from the West—Vancouver and Denver.

Few teams, it seemed, coveted Van Horn more than the Denver Nuggets, whose new Vice President for Basketball Operations Allan Bristow made no secret of his belief that Van Horn would be an All-Star for most of his NBA career. Denver, though, had the fifth pick in the first round. Philadelphia had the second pick, Boston the third, Vancouver the fourth.

Then there were the NBA champion Chicago Bulls, who had the very last pick in the draft, but hadn't yet committed to the roster that had won a fifth title in the decade of the nineties just a few weeks before the draft. They were looking to make some changes that might solidify their future in the post–Michael Jordan era, and they saw Van Horn as a piece of that puzzle, if only indirectly.

Boston Coach Rick Pitino, coming out of the college ranks himself, also openly coveted Van Horn, calling him a future superstar.

"We played him twice in college [when Pitino was head coach at the University of Kentucky] and I scouted him, but then when I worked him out, I thought he was going to be a future superstar in the NBA. First of all, he's legitimately 6–10 and a half. He runs like a three man. He can jump. He's a good passer. He has great one-on-one moves. He's a 90 percent foul shooter. So you're looking at somebody who shoots like [Larry] Bird. He doesn't have the passing skills of Bird, but as far as running, shooting, jumping, he's got it all."

All Pitino had to do to make certain he could get this future superstar was to make a deal that would move him up one spot in the draft order. With San Antonio certain to take Duncan, he could make Van Horn the number-two pick, if only he could get that pick away from Philadelphia. And he tried. So did Denver. So did others.

But ultimately, new Philadelphia 76ers Coach-Vice President of Basketball Operations Larry Brown and New Jersey Nets Coach-President of Basketball Operations John Calipari, whose team had the seventh pick in the first round, agreed on a multiplayer deal that went like this: Nets starters Jim Jackson and Eric Montross, plus the seventh pick of the first round (who would turn out to be Villanova's Tim Thomas) and the 21st pick of the first round (who would turn out to be Anthony Parker of Bradley), to Philadelphia in exchange for the draft rights to Van Horn, plus veteran center Michael Cage, forward Don MacLean, and guard Lucious Harris.

"We made several efforts to acquire him," Nets General Manager John Nash would say later. "John [Calipari] was very discouraged. We were pretty much set to wait at number seven and take Tim Thomas."

Ultimately, the Nets were willing to sweeten their bid to the 76ers from their original offer, which was just Jackson and Montross. So on draft night Van Horn donned a Philadelphia 76ers baseball cap when he was introduced as the second pick in the draft at Charlotte Coliseum, but everyone watching the proceedings on TV quickly learned he had been dealt to the Nets. Van Horn knew little about the Nets, and admitted it.

"I really didn't know anything about the Nets," he said. "I knew Dr. J [Julius Erving] had played there and they won a championship back in the ABA. I really didn't know much about New Jersey, either. After I knew I was going there, I had to look at a map and see where it was. I hadn't taken geography since the seventh grade. I lived on the West Coast all my life. I really didn't even know where it was. I mean, I knew it was next to New York. But I didn't know which side."

When he got to New Jersey, geography was the least of his concerns. Van Horn knew he would have to convince New Jersey fans, among the toughest in the NBA, he was worth the deal the Nets made to get him.

He had an inauspicious start. Less than two weeks after the draft, Van Horn appeared in Lodi, New Jersey, on behalf of his new team, which was building much of its ticket campaign around its prize rookie. Van Horn was asked to shoot some three-pointers in the parking lot of the semi-famous Bendix Diner. With trucks speeding by on the nearby turnpike, and a stiff breeze blowing in the parking lot, Van Horn went oh-for-appearance from long range.

It was hardly the way to sell season tickets,

or to begin your relationship with people you were trying to win over as your new fans.

Nets star Jayson Williams, one of the NBA's best rebounders, had decided to stop by the diner to see Van Horn for himself. Fortunately, Williams is one of the NBA's most loquacious players, and reporters on hand for Van Horn's display spent most of their time getting quotes from the veteran center-forward and paid little attention to Van Horn and his dismal shooting display. Williams paid no attention to the dismal shooting, either. He already had seen Van Horn work out, and he knew what kind of player he was going to be.

"I saw him hit 23 of 29 three-point shots, and then he goes in for the last one and dunks. I said, 'Whoa, I've got to make up with Cal.'"

Williams had been at odds with Calipari much of the previous season, Calipari's first on the New Jersey bench. But the thought of playing alongside Van Horn renewed Williams's desire to remain a Net.

"He is the best rookie to come into the league since Michael Jordan," Williams would tell reporters during the exhibition season, "and I've got 60,000 square feet of house to back that up."

Trouble was, Van Horn would not get to have the kind of start that might have made believers out of anyone skeptical of Williams's sanity when he called Van Horn the best rookie since Jordan. Late in the exhibition season, Van Horn suffered a severely sprained right ankle, an injury that would cost him the first 17 games of the regular season. It would be merely the first of several injuries Van Horn would have to cope with during a rookie season when he was supposed to challenge Duncan for Rookie of the Year honors, but did not.

Still, Van Horn tried to turn the negative experience into a positive. "I was able to learn a lot of things about the game that I wouldn't have had I just been thrown in. It was kind of a blessing because the team was doing pretty well. I was able to work on my strength, which I think has helped me a lot. I tried to turn it into a positive and watch and learn."

Williams never wavered in his praise of Van Horn, and the two became good friends. They were so at ease with one another that they became comfortable teasing each other about the most sensitive things, including race. After one spectacular move in a game, Williams even told reporters that he was going to make Van Horn wear an Afro next year.

Williams quit joking, however, when Detroit's Brian Williams, who is African-American, suggested that Van Horn was getting favorable treatment from referees because he was white. Brian Williams was upset because Van Horn had bloodied his lip while going for a rebound and no foul was called. Later, Williams said that if he got into a pickup game with Van Horn and no referees were present, he would pay him back.

That's when Jayson Williams jumped in to defend his teammate. "Brian ain't paying nothing back," he said, "I guarantee you that. Please don't make this out that I am going to beat up Brian Williams. Brian is a friend of mine. But I am not going to let anybody mess with Keith. I am not going to let anything happen to 'the franchise.'"

Van Horn, for one, did not care for the discussion on race. "People are going to say what they want to say," he said. "I don't get concerned with what other people are saying. He [Brian Williams] is the first person, really. It doesn't cross my mind. I don't get concerned. I just let it go. I don't think about it. I just go play my game."

Had Brian Williams implied that Van Horn was getting preferential treatment from the referees because of his star staus, Van Horn would have been willing to accept that. But that was far from the case. He was frequently in foul trouble, which is a common trait of rookies, who spend their first season earning respect from NBA referees.

"I've fouled out of almost every game I've played this year," he said, "so I'm not getting the calls. Officials should call fouls if they're fouls, and if they're not, they shouldn't call them. That's what they're there for. They shouldn't make a call based on [the fact] that I'm a rookie. It shouldn't matter. There shouldn't be any favoritism either way."

Van Horn couldn't escape the comparisons to Larry Bird, either. They were flattering, of course, but unfair.

"I said it when I was drafted," he said, "and I still feel the same way: It's unfair to compare me to Larry Bird. He's a Hall of Famer. I'm a rookie. I haven't accomplished anything yet. It's unfair, not only to myself, but to him. He's a legend. What have I accomplished?"

By the All-Star break, though, Van Horn had accomplished plenty. He was averaging 19.5 points and 6.0 rebounds, and he had become a clutch player, unafraid to take the shot with the game on the line. He was selected to play in the Schick Rookie Game on All-Star Saturday at Madison Square Garden, which might have been a bigger honor had Duncan, his prime competition for Rookie of the Year, not been selected to play for the Western Conference in the All-Star Game, the only rookie so honored.

Van Horn scored 17 points and grabbed a game-high 10 rebounds for the victorious Eastern Conference squad in the rookie game. He enjoyed the weekend, but his preference for a slower pace showed in the Big Apple.

"The only way I can describe it is wild," he said of the weekend experience, including the crush of people attracted wherever an NBA event was held during the weekend. "It's crazy. I didn't realize how big the NBA was until I walked into the hotel lobby and saw all those people."

Things were looking great for Van Horn and the Nets after the All-Star Weekend. In large part because of the rookie's impact, the Nets had a 27–21 record at the break and were in position to make a push for one of the top four spots in the Eastern Conference, a possibility not even their most ardent supporters could have imagined before the season began.

Bad luck, though, conspired with a brutal schedule to slow New Jersey's progress. Williams, the team's lone All-Star and its emotional leader, suffered a series of injuries that cost him 16 games in the final two months of the season, and he wasn't the only injured Net. Sam Cassell, Kendall Gill, and Kerry Kittles all missed games and Van Horn hit the infamous "Rookie Wall."

The Rookie Wall can't be seen, but its impact can be felt. Young players accustomed to playing no more than 30 or 32 games in a season, rarely more than two games a week, find themselves coping with the rigors of an eight-game exhibition season, followed by an 82-game regular season that usually has four games on a weekly schedule. There are road trips that last 10 days and longer, and take teams to as many as six different cities. Many a rookie, especially those who play big minutes, as Van Horn did, run out of gas shortly after the All-Star Game.

All season long, Van Horn shunned talk of the Wall, but when he shot a horrid 26.6 percent from the floor over a six-game stretch in late February, he had to admit he had hit it.

"All year I said there wasn't a Wall," Van Horn said. "But then I hit it fast and I hit it hard."

No advice Calipari could give could help Van Horn avoid the physical effects of his first pro season, though Coach Cal tried to help, and even enlisted the help of some of Van Horn's teammates.

"You have to work through the Wall," Calipari said. "You get rid of the fatigue by working harder, forcing harder. If you don't work harder and back off, you fall deeper into the abyss. I'm trying to get the guys to talk to him about these things. Kerry [Kittles] went through this last year, and I worked extra with him to get him through it. I want him to talk to Keith about how working harder helped."

Theories abounded as to why Van Horn's shooting touch had disappeared.

"People have to leave him and let this boy play his game," continued Calipari. "He's not a total jump shooter. I think maybe the [coaching] staff is putting pressure on him to catch and shoot too quickly. He's got to create and get into a flow. Plus, give him off a day or so. Keith only played like 28, 30 minutes a game at Utah. And he only played 30 games. We already doubled that, and he's playing 40."

As big a problem as dead legs were to Van Horn, the loss of confidence that accompanied hitting the Wall was even bigger.

"It gets to you a little bit," Van Horn said, "because you're always reminded of it. But you have to clear your mind. It's all part of the business. It wasn't so much my shot as I wasn't finishing plays. I've never really been a player to depend on my jump shot. Some nights they're hitting. Some nights they're not going down, but I would say most of the shots I'm taking are within 10 feet of the basket. I have to get my legs under me a little more. A half-second is a big difference. It's the difference in making a shot and missing a shot."

Everyone offered advice.

"I listen to it all," he said, "take what's meaningful and ignore the rest."

Ultimately, the rookie decided he needed to get some more rest.

"It's that half-second missing, maybe not exploding, not having the quick feet you normally do," he said. "I've tried to rest, get off my legs during the day. With all the stuff, you do get run ragged a bit. Not only basketball, but all the media requests and stuff you do afterward. Who isn't tired?"

Extra rest worked. Van Horn regained his shooting touch, but the Nets continued to struggle, mostly because of their injuries.

"It's been nonstop all year," Van Horn said late in the season. "It bothers me a little bit because we'll never know what we could have been this year. We're going to have years to come, and we've improved this year. We progressed, and I think we're going to continue to improve, but I don't think we'll ever be able to realize our potential because of all the injuries we had this year. No matter what I say . . . when you lose key players, it hurts you."

At the end of the season, Duncan easily won the Schick Rookie of the Year Award, receiving 113 out of 116 votes. Despite his limited activity, Van Horn received three votes, which, considering Duncan's outstanding season, was a surprise. But Van Horn had proven his worth. He was a key player in the Nets making their first playoff appearance since 1994. And even though the Nets lost in the first round of the playoffs to the eventual champion Chicago Bulls, they gained valuable experience and they have great hopes for the future. And Keith Van Horn is a big reason for that.

four
The Teenager

When Tracy Lamar McGrady graduated from high school, he was determined to be successful at his chosen profession. In that sense, he was no different than any of his peers in his graduating class at Mt. Zion Christian Academy in Durham, North Carolina. There was, however, a major difference in how quickly the Mt. Zion seniors planned to reach the top of their respective professions. Unlike many of his classmates, McGrady had no plans to invest time in college. The thought of an apprenticeship was foreign to him. And while the concept of "paying dues" was acceptable to McGrady, it was only because he figured he already had.

In the corporate world, McGrady's career plans would be somewhat like going from high school to being the CEO of a major company—a kind of accelerated Bill Gates. But why not? McGrady personified a trend that had been extremely successful for rare individuals the previous two years. He was the best high school player in the country. The previous two had been Kevin Garnett and Kobe Bryant, and they had proven that the best of the youngest could compete in the rare air of the NBA.

McGrady's great expectations were revealed on draft night when the Toronto Raptors selected him as their number-one choice. The man drafting him was Toronto Executive Vice President Isiah Thomas, who had been selected as one of the 50 Greatest Players in NBA History after a distinguished career with the Detroit Pistons. McGrady was asked how it felt to have someone who had been so successful as an NBA player spend such a high draft choice on such a young player. The diplomatic answer, of course, would be for McGrady to say that it was an honor being chosen by a man who had won two titles, and that any time a future Hall of Fame player picked you, it had to make you feel good.

Instead, McGrady's reply was: "I guess he sees a lot of talent in me—a great player down the road who can help his team win some games."

McGrady had just turned 18. Was the statement merely innocent confidence? Or was McGrady so out of touch with the high level of competition in the NBA that his visions of grandeur were more like hallucinations?

The answer probably lies somewhere in between, but no one could blame McGrady. He was the ninth player selected in the draft, and many players picked after him had attended college for two, three, or four years. Besides, his role models were not Thomas, Magic Johnson, or Larry Bird. His were much more contemporary—Garnett and Bryant.

It was the marvelously talented 6–11 Garnett who had opened the floodgates of youth when he went straight from Chicago's Farragut Academy to the Minnesota Timberwolves in 1995 as the fifth selection of the draft. The following year, two high schoolers, Kobe Bryant and Jermaine O'Neal, had gone from preps to pros. Bryant, in particular, was highly acclaimed in his first year, and he was the 13th player selected in the 1996 Draft—four places *after* McGrady was picked a year later.

Garnett immediately found himself on a fast track to NBA success. He enjoyed a fine rookie season, and in 1996–97 helped lead the Timberwolves into the playoffs for the first time in franchise history. A few weeks after the 1997 Draft, he would sign a contract extension with the Timberwolves that would pay him reportedly in excess of $125 million. Bryant also excelled as a rookie with the Los Angeles Lakers, and in only his second season, he was so popular throughout the world that fans voted him to be a starter on the 1998 All-Star Team. And he was not yet even starting for the Lakers.

McGrady had no reason to believe his path would be any different.

A gangly 6–8, McGrady had a 40-inch vertical leap, excellent ball-handling skills and, obviously, a tremendous upside. The Raptors, in fact, had McGrady rated higher than the ninth best player. Even if they'd had a pick before number nine, they would have taken him. In fact, Thomas feared McGrady would be selected before the Raptors would draft. When he was still on the board, Thomas lifted his eyes to the heavens and said, "Thank you, God." He could not believe his team's good fortune.

"I didn't expect we'd be lucky enough to be able to get Tracy at nine," he said.

McGrady and the Raptors seemed a perfect fit. Toronto already had one of the youngest rosters in the NBA, and Damon Stoudamire had quickly become one of the top point guards in basketball—a young leader who could take McGrady under his wing and ease his transition to the pro game. And in Thomas the Raptors had a basketball operations chief who was, if not a father figure, certainly a big brother figure for the team's young players.

But all Thomas's plans—not just for McGrady, but for the Raptors—unraveled only three weeks into the regular season. Thomas had been negotiating to buy the Raptors, but when the deal fell through, he ultimately decided to leave and accept a position with NBC Sports. Once he left, little seemed to go right for McGrady. The team went through a 17-game losing streak;

Stoudamire was traded to Portland; Darrell Walker, whom Thomas had handpicked as head coach, resigned; and the team was sold to new owners. Lost somewhere in the shuffle was a teenager a long way from home, a stranger in a cold, snowy, strange land. The child had been left, figuratively, like a babe on a doorstep.

"That's pretty much how I saw it," McGrady said of his wrenching transition to life as a wage-earning adult. "Early on, there just wasn't much attention paid to me. Nobody explained anything to me. Nobody told me what I was doing right or what I was doing wrong."

There was no question McGrady had a physical maturity that suited the NBA. In an 11-minute period in the Raptors' second game of the season, McGrady scored eight points, several of them with electrifying dunks against Atlanta. It was too easy to forget he was just a few months removed from hanging out at the shopping mall, scraping up his change to play video games or perhaps buy a new pair of Air Jordans.

Soon enough, reality set in. McGrady struggled through the early part of his rookie season, as he tried to adjust to the pace and complexity of the NBA game. When he got playing time, he was uncertain where he should be on the court, and when he should be there. All his athletic ability couldn't compensate for being out of sync with the team's concepts. Almost inevitably, McGrady found himself in Walker's doghouse. Walker went so far as to say that if McGrady didn't shape up, he'd be shipped out of the league. It was not the kind of statement a very young player struggling to find his identity wanted to hear, and it was devastating to his confidence.

Walker, though, was expressing much of his own frustration. A second-year coach who never had been a head coach at any level before, he was not sure how to deal with his young player.

"To be frank with you, as an organization we haven't done a very good job with Tracy," said Glen Grunwald, who replaced Thomas as the Raptors' top basketball executive. "With all the turmoil, we were so caught up in the day-to-day crises. But Tracy handled it fairly well, far better than I would have when I was 18."

Once Butch Carter, who had been an assistant under Walker, took over as head coach on February 13, the Raptors began to stabilize. The team's record didn't improve, but Carter at least began to pay some attention to McGrady's needs. The rookie was promised 10 to 15 minutes every game, and told that he could earn even more playing time by demonstrating dedication and advancement. Raptors assistant coach Jim Thomas was assigned to work with McGrady before every game and after every practice.

"The way the scenario was set up earlier," said Carter, "I don't think it was good for Tracy. It wasn't set up for him to be successful. They basically drafted an 18-year-old and let him hang out to dry. No workouts. No classroom. No nothing."

It was in stark contrast to McGrady's days at Mt. Zion. There, life was as structured as school administrators could make it. McGrady was wrapped in an insulating, demanding— but comfortable—cocoon. A typical day at the high school began at 4:30 A.M. with a run up the steps at the football stadium at Duke University. Following breakfast, McGrady attended classes wearing a coat and tie; went to church meetings; ate lunch; practiced basketball; and then headed back to his coach's home for the night. No personal phones or TV were allowed. There was no dating.

The coach at Mt. Zion was Joel Hopkins, who had discovered McGrady on a recruiting trip to his hometown of Auburndale,

Florida. Hopkins made it clear early on that he would be demanding of McGrady.

"When I first came to his house and met him," Hopkins said, "I made him take his earrings out at the dinner table. I told him I was going to leave his house if he didn't take those earrings out. Those are for sissies."

McGrady was tactful enough not to point out to Hopkins that Michael Jordan, hardly a sissy, wears a diamond earring.

McGrady had been raised by a single parent, his mother, Melanise Williford. She worked as a hotel chambermaid, driving back and forth each day to her job in Tampa. Until he was in 11th grade, McGrady's favorite sport had been baseball, and he was a standout pitcher in high school. But his athletic future changed in the summer of 1996, when he attended the prestigious Adidas ABCD basketball camp in New Jersey and was named MVP.

During his senior season at Mt. Zion,

McGrady averaged 27.5 points and shot 56.4 percent from the field. He was named high school player of the year by *USA Today*. His future looked bright, in no small measure because of Hopkins's strict influence.

"I wasn't bad, because I've never been in trouble with the law," McGrady said, "but I didn't have respect for people. I didn't have any respect for anyone until I met Coach Hopkins. He's the main reason I am here today and why my dream of playing in the NBA is being fulfilled. Coach Hopkins is my backbone. He's behind me, 100 percent. If it wasn't for Coach Hopkins and God, this wouldn't be possible."

"This" meant a $50,000 Lexus, a $16,000 Rolex watch, a three-bedroom house for his grandmother in Winter Haven, Florida, another car and house for his absentee father, a car and home for his mother—and diamond earrings forbidden by Hopkins for himself.

"I'm just like any other 18-year-old," McGrady said. "I hang out with my friends. I like to play video games."

Other 18-year-olds, though, don't have three-year contracts worth millions of dollars. With his NBA riches, McGrady was able to entertain his friends in a luxury Toronto lakefront high-rise condominium that costs $2,000 a month; jet his best pals to New York for All-Star Weekend; and pay for all those video games at the mall. That trip for his friends to New York almost never happened, though. There would have been no reason to bring them to the Big Apple had he not been selected to play in the Schick Rookie Game. And until Cleveland's Derek Anderson was injured just days before All-Star Weekend, McGrady hadn't played well enough—hadn't played enough, period—to merit a spot in the game. His performance had been spotty, at best, due almost exclusively to the turmoil that had beset the Raptors and arrested

McGrady's NBA development. McGrady, however, acquitted himself well in the rookie game, scoring nine points in 10 minutes.

But then it was back to the season, and the Raptors continued to struggle. McGrady admitted to being increasingly depressed with his team's losing and his disappointing season, and he skipped an off-court workout in the middle of March. Carter knew he had a player at a crossroads.

"I had a talk with him and told him not to cheat himself," Carter said. "He tried to tell the trainers that he didn't want to do a workout. I told him, 'We're not going to cheat you now.' Everything good that's happened lately is because of the extra work he has done. We're not going to back off because there's 20 games left and he's thinking about going to Florida. And that's just human nature. He's a young kid thinking, 'I spent my winter up here, and the sun's shining down there.' It's like anybody this time of year and you're in college. What are you thinking about? Spring break. But there's no spring break in the NBA."

Carter's message was driven home by Bryant, whom McGrady counts among his friends, when the Lakers were in Toronto to play the Raptors in late March. Both players have endorsement deals with Adidas, and they went out to dinner together the night before their teams were to play. McGrady regards Bryant, the youngest player ever voted to start in the NBA All-Star Game, as something of a big brother. So when Bryant spoke, McGrady listened closely.

"I told him not to get down," Bryant said. "I told him he's got to keep working hard. You can't let the things that are going on around you or other people get in the way of working hard and improving your game."

McGrady took Bryant's advice to heart. "Kobe turned his life around last summer," McGrady said. "His rookie season wasn't that good, but he made it known he wants to be a positive person, both on and off the court. Kobe worked so hard on his game. He hired a personal trainer and was always on time for the sessions. No partying. I was thinking to myself, 'Man, he's going to be somebody.' I hope to make a big jump in my game in my second year, just like he did. I'm not saying I'm going to be an All-Star like him, but I'll be better than I was."

While that is an admirable goal, there was something even more appealing about that statement. McGrady, indeed, had gained considerable wisdom since draft night when he spoke of his talent and potential great-ness. Instead, he spoke of hard work and dedication and even qualified his potential, saying his hope was to simply get better.

But he didn't have to wait that long. Late in the season, with his minutes increasing, there were signs of tangible—sometimes eye-popping—improvement. Playing small forward rather than shooting guard, as he had earlier in the season, McGrady even flirted with a triple-double against the defending champion Bulls on March 22, when he scored 12 points, grabbed nine rebounds, and handed out eight assists. That performance seemed to herald a transformation. In the first six games of April, the final month of the season, McGrady averaged 11.8 points and 9.3 rebounds, outstanding numbers by anyone's standards.

"Tracy is showing some definite signs of maturity," Carter said. "His confidence has increased. He's not afraid any longer to be assertive."

The most noticeable change in his game was his willingness to take mid-range jump shots and make them consistently. He also showed he could finish on the fast break, and his passing skills and court sense improved dramatically. He also began to use his unquestioned athleticism under the boards at the offensive end of the court.

The key for the youngest player in the NBA in 1998–99 will be to hang on to his improvements, and add to them in the off-season. To that end, McGrady was delighted when the Raptors in February traded for veteran guard Dee Brown, whose off-season home in Florida is a half hour from McGrady's. They planned to train together and work on their games all summer.

"He's got a lot to learn about taking care of yourself," Brown said. "Hopefully, he's going to be curious and dedicated."

five

The Aussie

When the time came for the Portland Trail
Blazers to make their selection in the first
round of the 1997 NBA Draft at Charlotte
Coliseum, they knew they would be selecting a relatively unknown player—and they
knew they would be selecting that player for
the Dallas Mavericks. Mavericks General
Manager Don Nelson had engineered a
draft-night trade, but with a deal-breaker
qualifier. The Mavericks would agree to give
up the 15th pick in the draft and take the
18th pick—along with a cash payment—but
only if Australian center Chris Anstey
remained on the draft board.

Nelson had surveyed the draft landscape after the lottery area, the first 13 picks, and decided to take something of a gamble. He knew he wanted Anstey, a 7–0 Australian who was starring for the South East Melbourne Magic of Australia's professional league, the National Basketball League (NBL). He figured he might be able to get Anstey later in the first round than the 15th pick, which the Mavericks owned. If a team holding the 16th or 17th pick selected Anstey at 16 or 17, Nelson's gamble wouldn't work.

When it came time for pick number 18, Anstey was still there. So Portland, at Nelson's instruction, chose Anstey, which elicited a curious "Who?" response from the crowd watching the draft in Charlotte, but Nelson knew who Anstey was. He had been scouting him for more than two years, and he believed that Anstey had exceptional natural ability.

Once the trade was announced a few minutes after Portland's selection, Nelson explained the pick to the Dallas media. In the process he made Anstey sound like the second coming of Bill Walton, Portland's Hall of Fame center from the 1970s.

"I like the fact that he's athletic," Nelson said of Anstey. "He can run, catch, pass, shoot, block shots, and rebound. There isn't a whole lot more to it, is there? And then he's 7–0. I envision he and Shawn Bradley playing together. We'll have a big front line when they do. He'll probably be the best running big man in the NBA. I haven't seen a 7-footer run the floor like he does. This was a guy we wanted. I'm not going to say this was the main guy, but I'm really happy we got him. He's not a project. He's ready to roll, as far as I'm concerned. As he gets stronger, he can play some backup center, some power forward, and some small forward."

How was it a young Australian who had first picked up a basketball only five years earlier found himself drawing such rave reviews from a man committed to paying him nearly $3 million over the next three seasons? Anstey had started out as a tennis player, one of the best young players in a tennis-crazy country. By the time he was 16, Anstey was 6–6 and one of the top-ranked junior tennis players in Australia. He had a booming left-handed serve to rival current Aussie net star Mark Philippoussis. But a growth spurt around his 19th birthday took him from 6–6 to 7–0, and his brother, Graeme, already hooked on basketball, introduced him to the game. Before long, Anstey was playing with the Melbourne Tigers, of the NBL. He backed up Australia's best big man, Mark Bradtke, who eventually would move to the NBA's Philadelphia 76ers.

After his rookie season with the Tigers, he signed with cross-town rival South East

Melbourne Magic, coached by Brian
Goorjian, a Californian who had played at
Pepperdine. Goorjian recognized Anstey's
potential and helped him develop it.
Anstey averaged 11.8 points and 7.8
rebounds as a second-year player, and
began to attract the attention of NBA
scouts when the Magic went on a six-game
tour of U.S. colleges after winning the NBL
championship. In an exhibition game
against eventual 1997 NCAA champion
Arizona, he scored 25 points and grabbed
10 rebounds. Nelson took note and began
following his career.

Anstey sat at his home in Melbourne and
watched the draft via satellite TV. Because of
the international date line and a 17-hour difference between Eastern Daylight Time and
the Melbourne time zone, it was June 26 in
Melbourne and June 25 in Charlotte. But the
only time that concerned Anstey was the time
it took to announce first-round selections. He

knew there was a chance he might be drafted in the first round—Nelson had told him the Mavericks were interested. But when it was time for the Mavericks to pick, they chose Iowa State's Kelvin Cato. Anstey then wondered what might happen, although he still believed he would be a first-round pick.

Some of the intrigue ended when the Blazers announced they had selected him, but that also caused confusion. He'd had no idea that the Blazers were interested. Still, he was pleased, and a few minutes later, his feeling turned into delight when Nelson called to tell Anstey the Mavericks had acquired his rights.

"I was just excited that I had finally been picked," Anstey said, "because I had a fair idea I was going to be picked in the first round. But when you see the draft [on television], you actually start to doubt what you've been hearing, and you think it only might happen. Right now I can't believe it finally happened. To be picked number 18 was fantastic and probably exceeded what I thought. It's a dream come true. It's a relief. Now I know where I'm going and I can make some plans. I'm happy. I didn't have any expectations or preferences, so I was going to be happy with wherever I went."

That would have included Portland, but the trade nullified that possibility.

"I hadn't heard any rumors," Anstey said of the deal that made him a Maverick, "but I had spoken to Dallas earlier in the day, and they said they were interested, but when they didn't pick me, I didn't know what was going to happen after that. My agent was back in New Jersey, and five minutes later he called me and I was back in Dallas. Obviously, I'm very excited."

So, what did he know of Dallas when he discovered it would be his basketball home?

"I didn't know a great deal about the team or the city," he said, "and I've never been there. I did know they had their big trade and they are in a rebuilding stage, and it's going to be fun to be part of that."

Anstey knew he was entering a brave new world of basketball, one where he no longer would be the biggest player on the floor. He tried to say the right things to the Dallas reporters who were linked to him on a draft-night conference call.

"Obviously, I have a lot of work to do," he told them. "I think I have pretty good feet for a person of my height, so I'm reasonably quick. I can also shoot pretty well for a person my height and can catch the ball and run the floor pretty hard. Those are the things I base my game on, and the longer I'm over there, the better I'll get. Obviously, it's going to be a bit of an adjustment. It's the best league in the world. Hopefully, I can improve my game before the season starts. There aren't a lot of 7-footers in Australia, so I know I'm in for a learning experience. This is the biggest, most physical, quickest league in the world. I have a lot to get ready for."

Ideally, Anstey would have begun getting ready for the NBA immediately, flying to Dallas from Melbourne. Except there was the matter of the NBL season, which was in its final weeks. But Anstey did not believe the Magic would stand in the way of his basketball progress.

"My club will not jeopardize that in any way," he said with confidence at the time. "I could be there next week, or it could be a month or two. But I'll be there."

Three weeks later, Anstey was indeed on a plane to Dallas, but he knew he would have to return to Australia to play the NBL season, per the contract he had with the Magic. His mission in Dallas: attend the Mavericks' minicamp, then head to Los Angeles for the annual Summer Pro-Am league, where he could hone his skills.

After a 26-hour flight that took him from

winter temperatures in the mid–40's in Melbourne to the 95-degree heat and matching humidity of a Texas summer, Anstey arrived on July 13 for mini-camp in Dallas, scheduled to begin two days later. Anstey was stunned to discover, on stepping into the terminal at Dallas/Fort Worth International Airport, that he was recognized immediately by a fan. A woman from Melbourne awaiting the arrival of her husband from Australia approached Anstey, gushing that she was a huge fan of the South East Melbourne Magic, the team Anstey played for in Australia's NBL. Anstey signed his first autograph in the United States and marveled. "I couldn't believe it," he said.

One of the first things he discovered on arrival at the Mavericks' headquarters was that the number he had worn for the Magic, his lucky number 13, already was taken on the Mavericks. Martin Muursepp had staked his claim to it, and in the NBA seniority rules when it comes to numbers. One of Anstey's first official responsibilities after arriving in Dallas was to attend a press conference for local reporters. He told them how excited he was to be a Maverick, to be part of the NBA.

"I have only been here a day," he said, "and so far it has been fantastic. The guys have been really great toward me. It's an exciting time for me. I'm looking forward to playing in the summer league in L.A., and when I come back here, I will hopefully get to meet more people and get out in the community. I'll try to settle down a little bit, so I'll be ready to go when I come back in October. Hopefully, I can pick up as much as I can in these next two weeks. The whole thing is a big-time learning experience for me. I'm just going to put in the time and effort and hopefully be ready by the time the season starts. First and foremost, I have to get stronger. I need to hit the weight room really hard. It's a different style of game. It is a quicker game. There is a 24-second clock. I'm used to a 30-second clock. Little things like that. I think I can make those adjustments. Every time I step on the court I'm going to be learning. The more time I can spend here learning, the quicker I can make those adjustments."

For all his sincere belief that the Magic never would stand in his way of making it to Mavericks training camp on time, Anstey discovered his Australian team was less than accommodating to that desire. After paying a higher price to buy Anstey out of his contract with the Magic than Nelson felt was fair, the Mavericks finally agreed to let Anstey finish out the Australian season. In turn, the Mavericks would have no financial obligation to the Australian team.

But Anstey's skills worked against him and the Mavericks—at least at that point. Because of his presence, the Magic ended up in the NBL finals. That meant Anstey missed Dallas's entire training camp and all eight preseason games.

"I guess the better we do over here," Anstey said from Australia, "the worse it is for me over there. It's obviously tough, but hopefully I'm not missing too much of the season. I hope the only part I really miss is the fitness work."

Finally, after a disappointing NBL finals series, where he suffered an ankle sprain and the Magic lost to his old team, the Melbourne Tigers, Anstey arrived in Dallas to begin his NBA career. It was November 3, and the Mavericks were off to a 2–0 start that included a stunning victory in Seattle over the SuperSonics, who would eventually win 61 games. "It's great," Anstey said of his new team's start. "We better not start losing, or I'll be blamed for it."

But the Mavericks did start losing . . . and losing . . . and losing. And Anstey soon discovered that raw potential, mixed with unfamiliarity with a new team's philosophy of play, resulted in massive bench time. After he joined the team he jumped into practice with his new teammates, but his first game with the Mavericks was the same as his last experience with the Magic—a loss. Although Dallas had beaten the Vancouver Grizzlies on the road in the season opener and followed that with the stunning SuperSonics upset, the very next night the Mavericks couldn't beat the Grizzlies on their Reunion Arena floor in front of fans who had patiently stuck with a team that has had the worst record in the NBA through the decade of the 1990s. Anstey, however, didn't get off the bench all night, except to cheer his new teammates. Coach Jim Cleamons obviously felt he wasn't quite ready for the demands of a real NBA game.

Anstey stayed on the bench the next night when he suited up for his first road game as an NBA player, in the same Charlotte Coliseum where he had been chosen in the draft. Back in Dallas three nights later, on November 8, Anstey finally would make his NBA debut, becoming the fifth native-born Australian to play in the world's best league, after Andrew Gaze, Luc Longley, Shane Heal, and Mark Bradtke.

It was an inauspicious debut. In two minutes of court time, Anstey didn't attempt a shot, either from the field or the foul line, grabbed only one rebound, blocked one shot, turned the ball over once, and committed one foul. And the Mavericks lost the game. In his second game, Anstey was introduced to NBA post play by the game's most powerful player. The Los Angeles Lakers' 7–1, 315-pound center Shaquille O'Neal caught Anstey above the right eye with an elbow as the two battled for a rebound, and Anstey retired to the training room to take five stitches to close the wound.

It would be more than a week before Anstey would score his first NBA points, getting a dunk against the Trail Blazers at the Rose Garden in Portland on November 17. It was his longest stint of the season, 12 minutes of a blowout loss as Dallas would begin a long slide that eventually would get Cleamons fired, replaced on the bench by Nelson, the man who had engineered the trade for Anstey with such high hopes for the big man from Down Under. It was apparent that Cleamons had little faith in Anstey's ability to play the pivot against the powerful big men of the NBA. He rarely used him unless a game was well beyond the critical stages when it would still be won or lost, saving him for what's known in the NBA as "garbage time," in the fourth quarter. Through the first month of the season, the big rookie had played in only seven of 15 games. His first season was going to be a big-time—but also disappointing—learning experience.

One of those lessons occurred quickly. On December 4, Anstey got a firsthand lesson in business realities of the NBA. Only 16 games into the season, Cleamons was fired. Nelson, who had steadfastly professed that he never would return to the bench, took over on the morning of December 4, then directed the fired-up Mavericks to a 105–91 win at Reunion Arena that night over the New York Knicks, a team that had fired him two years earlier.

It was enough of a blowout win that Nelson could afford to play Anstey the final four minutes of the game, which was only the second time Anstey had played in a game the Mavericks won. But he soon would discover that while Nelson may have said on draft day that Anstey was not a project, when it came time to play, Nelson treated Anstey that way. Anstey was not getting any more playing time under Nelson than he did under Cleamons, and then five games after Nelson took over, Anstey suffered an ankle injury that would keep him on the shelf for a long while.

Already, Anstey had discovered how difficult it was going to be to score against the NBA's quick big men. Through his first 16 NBA games, more often than not, his statistical line at the end of games read: DNP-CD (Did Not Play-Coach's Decision). During that time his grand totals were 17 points scored while making only seven of the 21 shots that he attempted. What he did show, on occasion, was an ability to rebound and run the floor, but Nelson obviously had no intention of letting him play his way into a comfort zone. When Nelson was asked, in late December, why Anstey hadn't played since December 18, his response chilled Anstey to the bone.

"Because," Nelson said, "I don't want him to become a laughingstock."

This, from a man who had predicted Anstey would become the best running big man in the NBA, was a cold shot to the heart, even though Nelson said he was looking out for Anstey's long-term interests by protecting confidence that was in short supply. Anstey tried to respond to Nelson's harsh comments in as positive a way as he could. He had tried hard not to believe Nelson's hype, that "best running big man" exaggeration, when he had arrived in Dallas, and he tried to maintain perspective about the "laughingstock" comment now.

"I made that mistake once before," Anstey said of listening to those who predicted great things for him. "The Australian media built me up to be some superstar in the making, and I wasn't ready for that. It took me awhile to come back down to earth. Now I don't worry about expectations. I played four minutes a game my first year [in Australia's NBL]. The next year, I played 15 minutes a game. Last year [the 1997 NBL season], was the first year I actually played heavy minutes, so I know exactly what it's like. This season is definitely not discouraging. It's more like familiar territory."

On January 2, Anstey badly sprained his left ankle in a practice session in Dallas and immediately was placed on the injured list. He would remain on the list until January 17, but would not play until January 30. He used this forced hiatus from the game to commence a turnaround from rookie failure. About the same time Nelson told the media Anstey was too raw and too weak for the NBA, Nelson, one of the NBA's veteran coaches and personnel chiefs, told Anstey the only way he would make himself into an NBA player was to hit the weight room with enthusiasm and dedication. And that's what he did when he was forced to the sidelines by the sprained ankle, becoming a constant companion of Mavericks assistant strength coach Chad Lewis, who began molding his body into something resembling an NBA frame. He also began working daily on his

post moves with Mavericks scout Mark
Aguirre, who was the first major star in
Dallas history during the 1980s, and team-
mate Kurt Thomas.

Finally, after Anstey returned to the floor
in late January his dedication to strength and
conditioning began to pay off. In 21 minutes
of a 110–99 loss to the Celtics at Boston's
FleetCenter on February 4, Anstey scored 12
points and grabbed eight rebounds. His performance was impressive enough that Nelson
reconsidered his regular playing rotation
and penciled in Anstey's name.

"I like what I see," Nelson said. "I'm comfortable with Chris on the floor. But he has
to have a very active summer. He has to be
involved in all our summer programs and
not spend much time in Australia, and then
we'll see what we have next year."

Those were encouraging words to Anstey,
who began getting more and more playing
time. After the All-Star break, Anstey played

in 21 consecutive games, finally beginning to live up to the hype that had contributed to the early and unfair perception that he had been a draft-day bust. And he picked the right time to blossom, because on March 12 he lived a dream nobody could have envisioned when he left Australia for Dallas four months earlier. Scoring eight points, including two in overtime, Anstey helped the Mavericks, with one of the worst records in the NBA, defeat Michael Jordan and the Chicago Bulls, the two-time defending NBA champions who would go on to capture their third consecutive title and sixth overall in June.

How the Mavericks won was even more astounding than the fact that they did. Down 17 with nine minutes left in regulation time, and down 10 with only 1:19 remaining, Dallas rallied to tie the score, then easily won the game in overtime 104–97. It was the highlight of Anstey's up-and-down season. Not only had he made a tangible contribution to the Mavericks' biggest victory of the entire season, he had done it against the Bulls and Luc Longley, the fellow Australian who mans the pivot spot for the Bulls, the most successful Aussie basketball player ever in the NBA. And a stare-down with Chicago's notorious rebounder and resident free spirit Dennis Rodman added to the growing affection Mavericks fans were developing for their rookie.

The Mavericks had taken a seven-point lead in overtime when Anstey beat Rodman to a rebound under the Bulls' basket, with Rodman doing his physical best to get the precious basketball away from the audacious Aussie. Anstey was having none of Rodman's attempts to intimidate. Slowly putting an elbow against Rodman's neck, he stared down a player who has made a career of intimidating bigger opponents in the paint. Both players broke into grins as the stare-down continued. Rodman grabbed

Anstey around the waist and gave him a tiny hug, a show of respect for a youngster who had dared to stand up to him.

The Reunion Arena crowd roared in approval.

And going against Jordan and beating him was the most delicious experience in a young career.

"It was the kind of thing that every young kid dreams of doing," Anstey said, "playing against Michael Jordan and beating him. It was incredible, in that not only were we down 17 in the fourth quarter with nine minutes to go, but also down 10 with 1:19 to go."

Afterward, Longley congratulated his countryman and offered some advice.

"His main advice," Anstey said, "was just 'Keep your head up. It's always harder at the start, both being away from home and being new in the league. Just keep working hard and let everyone know you're working hard, because the results will come.'"

Longley had chosen a different path to the NBA than Anstey. He had attended the University of New Mexico and honed both his basketball skills and his body under the tutelage of Americans with a clearer understanding of what it takes to make it in the NBA. But it still took Longley awhile to develop into the contributing player he has become with the Bulls, a fact Anstey finds encouraging. Longley had four years to adjust to life in America, too, whereas Anstey had to make an instant transition. Along the way he found he missed his homeland, some things more than others.

"When it comes to something Australian," Anstey said, "I would say fish and chips . . . and tennis."

Playing on a regular basis helped him get over his homesickness. Anstey was a regular in Nelson's playing rotation from January 30 through March 21, playing in 26 consecutive games before spraining the middle finger on his left hand in a game against the Houston Rockets. On March 7, against the Miami Heat at home, he played 34 minutes, his longest stint to date of the season and the kind of playing time NBA starters merit. Then on March 17 against Boston—the team that he had made something of a rookie season breakthrough against on February 4— Anstey had his finest night. In 38 spectacular minutes he made 11 of 15 shots, four of six free throws, scored 26 points, grabbed eight rebounds, had two steals, and blocked a shot in Dallas's 99–93 win.

Late in the game, the outcome still in doubt, Anstey blocked Walter McCarty's three-point shot attempt, preserving the Mavericks' victory. He was the man of the hour, and it was oh, so special, for in the Reunion Arena crowd were his parents, Ken and Anne, who had recently arrived in Texas to see their son play in the NBA. And it was Anne Anstey's birthday.

"It turned out to be a pretty good day for Mom," Chris Anstey said.

Most of the Celtics remembered Anstey from the earlier game in Boston, but in the meantime they had traded for point guard Kenny Anderson. After the game Anderson literally didn't know what had hit his team.

"Never heard of him," the veteran point guard said. "We played them twice when I was with Portland, and I don't remember him."

Why would he? The two games that Anderson referred to were in the first two weeks of the season, when Anstey was a complete afterthought for Cleamons. Afterward, Anstey reflected on how far he had come since those games against Portland in November.

"It was the work I did when I wasn't playing," he said by way of explaining his breakout game. "It's starting to pay off. Everyone is getting more comfortable with me, and

I'm feeling more comfortable on the court. Put those two things together and I think I'm improving. But I'm not surprised because I know what I can do."

The season had come full circle for a rookie nobody in Dallas had heard of back in June, when Nelson traded for Anstey and pronounced he would be one of the league's best big men. Anstey had arrived in Dallas to expectations raised prematurely and nearly guaranteeing failure; had been called a flop by the same man who had predicted such unlikely greatness; and finally had shown the promise that had given rise to such unfair projections in the first place.

While Anstey would finish the season on the injured list after spraining his right thumb on April 9, he would head into the off-season knowing the confidence he had inspired in Nelson back on June 25 had not been misplaced. Now he understood the key to unlocking the door to that potential that had so intrigued his boss. A few days after season's end, he boarded a plane for the 26-hour trip back to Melbourne, secure in the knowledge he belonged in the NBA, a rookie no more.

six
The Poet

Two roads diverged in a yellow wood,
And sorry I could not travel both
And be one traveler, long I stood
And looked down one as far as I could
To where it bent in the undergrowth;
Then took the other, as just as fair,
And having perhaps the better claim,
Because it was grassy and wanted wear;
Though as for that the passing there
Had worn them really about the same,
And both that morning equally lay
In leaves no step had trodden black.
Oh, I kept the first for another day!
Yet knowing how way leads on to way,
I doubted if I should ever come back.

I shall be telling this with a sigh
Somewhere ages and ages hence:
Two roads diverged in a wood, and I —
I took the one less traveled by,
And that has made all the difference.
　　—Robert Frost, "The Road Not Taken"

The road most traveled in today's world of multimillion-dollar pro sports contracts leads gifted young basketball players to the NBA without benefit of four years of college experience. Some choose the league without spending a single day in college, which is the path chosen by Tracy McGrady, who went directly to the Toronto Raptors from Mt. Zion Christian Academy.

When Jacque Vaughn completed his junior season at the University of Kansas, there were friends and advisers urging him to rush for the riches of the NBA, but Vaughn is a poet, and he was inspired by one of America's greatest writers of verse to remain in college. When he made that decision, he knew he was choosing the road less traveled, and for Vaughn it has made all the difference—at least in terms of maturity, which has endeared him to coaches and teammates alike. What Vaughn went through his rookie year might have caused a younger player to pout, or become depressed. Indeed, if a younger player was drafted by a team that had one of the 50 Greatest Players in NBA History as a starter at his position, and another up-and-coming pro only a few years older than Vaughn backing up the legend at the position, the rookie could be perplexed, befuddled, and upset.

But Vaughn was able to adapt to his circumstances when they were good, accept his station in life when idle, provide support, demonstrate a great attitude, and help to make sure that a positive situation was not poisoned by individual desires. Jacque Vaughn, in short, entered the NBA as a grown-up, and although he would never criticize a younger player for wanting the money, an education and four years in college worked for him.

This even takes into account that fate was cruel to him after he made his decision to stay at Kansas for his senior season. In the fall of 1996 before official practices began, Vaughn fell during a pickup game, and when he tried to brace his fall, he tore the major ligament in his right wrist, the one attached to his shooting hand. It was an injury similar to the one suffered in December 1997 by Patrick Ewing, who returned to play five months later. It was the worst kind of injury for a point guard, and Vaughn was advised by the doctor who performed surgery on the wrist to sit out the season because he wouldn't be able to play effectively if he tried to return too soon.

But, as Ewing would later do, Vaughn chose his own path, which was to throw himself into a vigorous program of physical rehabilitation, and he miraculously returned to play for the Jayhawks 11 games into Kansas' season. The injury did limit his effectiveness, however, and by the time the 1997 NBA Draft arrived in June, Vaughn was not listed among the top prospects, not even among the top four point guards.

On draft night he waited at his parents' home in Los Angeles as team after team passed him by. Point guards went early, and often: Chauncey Billups of Big 12 Conference rival Colorado, the third pick of the first round, to the Boston Celtics; Antonio Daniels of Bowling Green, fourth, to Vancouver; Brevin Knight of Stanford, 16th, to Cleveland; Bobby Jackson of Minnesota, 23rd, to Seattle (and on to Denver in a draft-night trade). Just when Vaughn began to believe he would not be taken in the first round, the Utah Jazz, a team with one of the greatest point guards in NBA history still on its roster in John Stockton, and a solid backup in Howard Eisley, to boot, made Vaughn the 27th selection of the 1997 Draft. Vaughn let out a deep sigh of relief . . . and smiled.

"Big smile," Vaughn said. "That was the first thing. A big smile came on my face. I am a huge NBA fan, and I have always felt that the Utah Jazz is a great team, as far as the players who are there, the success that they have. I was just glad I was going to be a part of it."

When the Jazz drafted Stockton in 1984, team executives heard he was too small to become a big-time star in the NBA. When the Jazz drafted Karl Malone a year later, they heard he didn't shoot well enough to become a dominant force in professional basketball. Maybe that's why the Jazz brain trust did not concern themselves with the reasons 26 other teams passed on Vaughn in the 1997 Draft.

Too small? Can't shoot?

No problem.

Those were the raps on Vaughn, who stands only 6–1, same as Stockton, who is bound for the Naismith Memorial Basketball Hall of Fame when he finally retires from the game. The Jazz jumped at the chance to take Vaughn, even though Stockton and Eisley already formed one of the most dependable point-guard combinations in the league. Utah's thinking? Stockton and Eisley would play in the games, while Eisley and Vaughn would get most of the practice time, saving considerable wear and tear on the 35-year-old Stockton's body.

All the while Utah would get a possible glimpse of the future—life without Stockton, which might not be so daunting should Eisley and Vaughn prove to be an able one-two punch. Of course, Vaughn knew nothing of the Jazz's plans as he watched the draft with friends and family in Los Angeles. He never dreamed he would slip all the way to Utah, picking 27th, and he certainly didn't expect he would end up going to a team that already seemed to have all the point guards it needed.

Vaughn had tried to prepare himself for any eventuality on draft night. He never told anyone there was a certain place where he would prefer to play. And he had played well enough at the Desert Classic in Phoenix, a tournament conducted strictly for the benefit of pro scouts, to believe he would be gone before Utah selected.

"I thought," Vaughn said, "I was pretty well prepared for any scenario." But on draft night, as each team passed on him, he began to get anxious, even a bit depressed. "After the 15th or 16th pick," he said, "I just sat back . . . and watched. A couple of players went higher than expected. That pushed me down, I guess."

While Vaughn was bewildered and sad as each team passed him by, Utah Vice President of Basketball Operations Scott Layden got more and more excited. And when it came time for the Jazz to pick, Layden didn't hesitate. "We were surprised Jacque was still around," he said. "We didn't expect it, not at all. We liked him all along. Why other teams didn't, I can't say."

After Vaughn finished smiling, he began assessing his new team. "My first thought was, 'This could be a great opportunity for me,'" Vaughn said. "I was enthused at the idea of going to Utah."

Without question Vaughn had dropped in the draft in part because of questions pro scouts had about his perimeter shot. The torn wrist ligament had affected it. He had led the Big 12 Conference in three-point shooting as a junior, when many were predicting he would be an NBA lottery draft pick, but in his senior season he became more of a distributor of the ball, getting it to talented teammates like Raef LaFrentz and Paul Pierce. "I didn't get to shoot the ball," he recalled.

Vaughn signed his rookie contract in July and went to the Jazz's rookie camp, then to the Rocky Mountain Revue, where he would get his first chance to play in the Delta Center. Although San Antonio's eventual Rookie of the Year Tim Duncan was on the Spurs' team at the tournament, Vaughn was the object of the most scrutiny, playing in front of what would become his home-team fans. In general, the reviews were good. But the Utah fans had the luxury of judging Vaughn only as a third guard. There was no way he was going to displace Stockton, and Eisley had been deemed a valuable player by the Jazz and head coach Jerry Sloan, who usually favors experience over promise. None of this was bad for Vaughn. He would be able to learn slowly, under the masterful tutelage of Stockton, and he also would have very competitive practices with Eisley.

During the preseason, however, Vaughn's role changed. Stockton suffered the first serious injury of his stellar 14-year career, an injury to his right knee that required surgery. After playing in 609 consecutive regular season games, Stockton began the season on the injured list. Suddenly, Vaughn was thrown into Sloan's regular playing rotation.

"Ready or not," Vaughn said, "I was thrust into the fire. But it's something that will benefit me later on in my career."

Vaughn proved to be a lot more ready than anyone could have predicted. Through the first 18 games, which Stockton missed, Vaughn averaged 4.8 points and 3.6 assists, and helped direct one of the NBA's most

precise half court offenses. He also kept the
Jazz running, at the insistence of Sloan. "He
did a wonderful job," Sloan said. "He paid
attention; he listened; and he got better and
better."

Among other things, Vaughn proved he
could defend at the NBA level. In the first
week of his NBA career, in only his third
game, he found himself matched up with
Washington Wizards point guard Rod
Strickland, who eventually would lead the
league in assists for the 1997–98 season. In
26 minutes of head-to-head play against
Strickland, Vaughn scored seven points and
handed out six assists. Strickland scored 17
points, but needed 20 shots to get them.
Vaughn gave no ground to one of the
league's best at penetrating the lane and
dishing to teammates. Of perhaps the greatest significance, Sloan chose to go with
Vaughn in the final minutes of a close
game, a crunch-time decision that showed

Tim Duncan's selection as San Antonio's top pick—and the top pick in the draft—was seen by many as the boost that would bring the Spurs a long-awaited NBA championship.

On and off the court, Duncan's transition to the pros was mentored by another big man in San Antonio, David Robinson.

All eyes were on Duncan at the 1998 NBA All-Star Game in Madison Square Garden, where he joined the league's elite players in the midseason classic.

Duncan attained the ultimate rookie honor by overwhelmingly winning the 1997–98 Schick Rookie of the Year Award. He would soon top that recognition when he was selected as a member of the All-NBA First Team.

ANDY HAYT

NOREN TROTMAN

Duncan and Robinson working against Utah in the Conference Semifinals. Utah won this game 83–82 and went on to eliminate the hopeful Spurs.

Keith Van Horn found a kindred spirit and mentor in Jayson Williams, who would become Van Horn's most vocal supporter.

Van Horn faced the kind of superstar competition young players only dream of: slamming against Scottie Pippen (*top*), driving against Michael Jordan (*middle*) and boxing out Shaquille O'Neal (*bottom*).

ANDY HAYT

Van Horn quickly became a fan-favorite in New Jersey and proved himself to be worthy of the high expectations heaped upon him.

TIM DeFRISCO

Rookie Jackson maneuvers against MVP Jordan.

NATHANIEL S. BUTLER

Bobby Jackson began his pro career on a struggling team, but that situation afforded him plenty of playing time—a rare commodity for other rookies.

Jacque Vaughn's first season took him straight to the coveted NBA Finals—a plateau many players never reach.

Vaughn crouches, ready to spring against a New York Knicks' attack.

Chris Anstey gets final instructions from Dallas Coach Don Nelson before checking into a game.

Anstey joined the ranks as one of the NBA's many international players, making the transition from Australian basketball.

NATHANIEL S. BUTLER

Straight out of high school, Tracy McGrady faced tall obstacles his first year in Toronto but enjoyed his first pro season overall.

NATHANIEL S. BUTLER

McGrady dunking against the New Jersey Nets— on his way to averaging a respectable seven points per game his rookie season.

what confidence one of the league's best coaches had in an untested rookie.

"It was a great experience," Vaughn said. "I got a feeling for what it's like to be in the game with two minutes left. And Rod, he was taking the approach of trying to take the game over. Everybody wants to be complimented by their peers, and afterward, Rod complimented me on the way I played."

Typical of Vaughn's team-oriented approach, though, he refused to find much comfort in his performance because Washington won the game, 90–86. On December 8, with the Indiana Pacers and their new coach, legendary Larry Bird, in town, Stockton returned from the injured list. It was a moment of exultation for the Jazz and their delirious fans, who greeted Stockton with a prolonged standing ovation when he entered the game for the first time. The Jazz won the game against one of the

Eastern Conference's best teams, 106–97, and Stockton led the team in assists, with seven. Vaughn knew his season had taken a dramatic turn. For the remainder of the year, his road to the court from the bench would be much less traveled.

"It was challenging," Vaughn said of the sudden elimination of nearly every opportunity to play. "The type of person I am, I want to be out there. I understood the situation, but it was certainly a test, mentally."

While the other point guards drafted in the first round were getting 25 to 35 minutes a game—even Jackson, who went just four picks ahead of Vaughn, was a starter for the Nuggets—Vaughn's playing time suddenly was limited to "garbage time." Vaughn did his best to look for the silver lining of a dark personal cloud.

"A lot of people asked me if I would prefer playing a lot more for a losing team," Vaughn said. "They say, 'Wouldn't you rather be in that situation?' But I answer them all quickly and easily, 'No.' I'm learning good habits here. I'm learning what the atmosphere should be like in an NBA locker room. I'm learning a winning approach to the game."

Sloan was impressed with the mental toughness and team-oriented attitude of his team's only rookie. "A lot of guys come into the league as starters and, being young guys, they make mistakes," said Sloan. "And they'll be making the same mistakes 10 years from now because they haven't had a chance to learn the game."

Unanimously, Vaughn's teammates praised his class after he was relegated to the number-three point-guard position, which rarely afforded the opportunity to play in meaningful minutes.

"He's a great young man," said Bryon Russell, a small forward who had gone from starter to reserve early in the season. "He's what a point guard should be. He doesn't make stupid decisions."

"Everyone on the team enjoys Jacque," said Shandon Anderson, another backup forward. "He wants to play, but he knows he's in a situation he can't control. So he's made the best of it."

Eisley, who admitted great surprise and skepticism when the Jazz had drafted Vaughn, was especially appreciative of Vaughn's mature acceptance of his situation.

"He's the type of person you want on your team," Eisley said. "He works hard every day. He has a great attitude. He tries to improve every time he steps on the court."

Stockton also watched Vaughn with an appreciative eye.

"I like a lot of things about him," said the Jazz's great point guard, who understood completely the cynicism many had about an undersized player with a suspect jumper, having walked in those very shoes after he was drafted to play behind Rickey Green in 1984. "He works on his days off. He's got a great approach to the game. Like everybody, he has a lot to learn. But he's smart, and he's learning all the time."

Nobody in basketball works harder on his game and his fitness than Utah's great power forward, Karl Malone, and he, too, gave Vaughn his stamp of approval.

"Jacque definitely has a future here," said the man known universally as The Mailman. "What I like most about him is he keeps his mouth shut and stays ready to play. He's always waiting for a chance to help the team. I have the utmost respect for him."

On the Jazz, that is the ultimate compliment. Along the way, during Vaughn's rookie season, his teammates began to notice that, during the team's flights on its charter aircraft to and from games, Vaughn would go off by himself with a notepad and write intently in it. What most of them didn't know was that Vaughn was writing poetry, pouring out his feelings on paper in a structure that allowed him to express his innermost thoughts.

He had come to poetry as a gradeschooler, when he memorized a poem a classmate had impressed him by reciting. He had been inspired not only by the fact of a young contemporary's ability to memorize the verse, but by its message.

"I don't know who wrote the poem," Vaughn said, "but I still remember it."

It went like this:

I've seen the daylight breaking high above
*   the bough.*
I've found my destination and I've made
*   my vow*
*   So whether you abhor me*
*   Or deride me or ignore me,*

Mighty mountains loom before me and I
   won't stop now.

It is a message Vaughn has taken with him the rest of his life. He would turn to poetry, which so many youngsters sarcastically deprecate, as a source of delight and inspiration.

"That was the start of my poetic life," Vaughn said. "It was just a curiosity thing at first, but I started to explore a little bit when I got into high school, and I used it to take my mind off everyday life and basketball, which I was playing seriously by then."

When he got to Kansas, he enrolled in courses that included the study of poetry, its structure and meaning.

"When I got to college," he said, "I used poetry for the same thing, but more so for enjoyment. I started writing poetry more in college and took some courses. Any time I had a chance to gain more knowledge about it, I took the opportunity. I also began to keep my own scrapbook, or journal, of things I've jotted down over the years."

Vaughn discovered the various forms of poetry, from Japanese haiku to Shake-spearean sonnets. He reveled in the beauty of words put together so magically as to make one cry. Along the way he discovered Robert Frost and then Maya Angelou, one of America's greatest living poets.

"I'm a huge fan of Maya Angelou, and I think there's some sort of connection, because of the type of person she is and what she has done with her life, knowing the history about her and the kind of tribu-lation she went through in her younger days, and the kind of person she has grown to today—a respected humanitarian—and the things she's been able to accomplish, simply because she had a task in life she wanted to accomplish.

"I think that [her life] sometimes reflects the way I look at life. I have a task in life, I think. I want to be successful in this league, and I work hard at what I do. So when I look at myself in the mirror every morning, I'm able to do that."

Angelou spoke at Kansas while Vaughn was there, and he went to hear her speak in her measured, flowing style. He left her speech with a new dream.

"I'd love to meet her sometime," he said. "You always get those questions, 'Who would you want to talk to before you die?' The answer for me is Maya Angelou. I'd love to sit down and have lunch and talk with her for an hour. I probably wouldn't talk. I'd just love to hear her talk. I would definitely ask her to recite a poem."

Vaughn continued to write poetry throughout his rookie season, despite occasional ribbing from teammates unused to such intellectual pursuits.

"It's a great way for me to have something personal," Vaughn said, "and while my life is somewhat public because I play the game of basketball, it's something I can hold on to, so those nights when we come home from a loss, and I'm getting home at three o'clock in the morning after a long flight after a road game, maybe I just need to read something, maybe I just need something to settle me so I can go to sleep. It's been a tough year for me, very mentally challenging and very tough for me because of the situation that I am in. [Poetry has] been something for me to have an outflow of expression in a positive way. So it's something I think is beneficial for me."

And always Vaughn returns to Frost, to "The Road Not Taken."

"That's something I read often," he said. "I have read a lot of Robert Frost's poems, and that has a special place in my mind, especially when my decision process was coming around. Not only was it influential at that time, when I was making my decision to stay at Kansas, but also right now in my life. I can easily say the situation I'm in, I could have taken a totally different approach than what I do. I think if you ask my teammates and my coaches, the approach I take, for many it would be, again, the road less traveled. Two roads are diverging again, and I have a choice of how I am going to approach the rest of my career, so it's definitely something that could be looked at in my life right now. The road less traveled."

seven

Bobby Jackson Revisited

It was a mere four games into his first season as a professional that Bobby Jackson began to feel anxiety about the short-term future of his team, the Denver Nuggets.

The Nuggets had played well in their first three games, including on opening night when Jackson poured in 27 points and stole most of the rookie thunder from San Antonio's Tim Duncan. But they had lost the game. The brutal reality of life in the NBA was awaiting the Nuggets at Denver International Airport, where a chartered jet was ready to take them to Salt Lake City.

There, 24 hours after playing his first game as a pro, Jackson would have to go up against the defending Western Conference champion Utah Jazz, making their regular season debut, rested and ready for a rookie-laden Nuggets team.

And exactly one week after the opener, who should the Nuggets be facing in their fourth game in eight days, this time at McNichols Sports Arena?

The Jazz again.

Through the first three games it was clear that Eric Williams, the third-year forward the Nuggets had acquired from the Boston Celtics during the summer, was perfectly suited to Coach Bill Hanzlik's up-tempo style of play. A slasher from the small forward position, Williams had a relentless style that induced opponents to foul him often. Williams's penchant for drawing fouls, which earned him numerous trips to the free throw line, was one element of his

superb overall offensive game. It was not difficult to project him averaging at least 20
points a game, something only 14 NBA players would do during the 1997–98 season.

Late in the third quarter against the Jazz,
Williams became entangled with reigning
Most Valuable Player Karl Malone under the
Utah basket and felt a twinge in his right
knee. Williams immediately left the floor
with trainer Jim Gillen and team doctor
Steven Traina. He was examined briefly in
the locker room, but told each man the
knee felt fine, and he wanted to go back in
the game.

In the fourth quarter Williams was back,
and he and Jackson nearly led the Nuggets
to an upset win over a team that would finish with the best record in the NBA. The
next morning, Williams awoke with a knee
puffed up nearly twice its normal size. The
diagnosis: torn anterior cruciate ligament,
the most serious of all knee injuries, and

one that would put him on the shelf for the remainder of the season.

The Nuggets—even the rookies—knew what Williams's loss would mean to a team so young, so desperately in need of every player who had proved capable of scoring the way Williams had shown he would. No team can lose a 20-point scorer and be successful. For a young team without a dominating center or power forward, the outlook was even worse.

The Nuggets were in deep trouble.

"When Eric went down," Jackson said, "that's when I first started to worry a little. Then Bryant [Stith] had to have another surgery, and then, all of a sudden, it seemed like we were in that 23-game losing streak. There were a lot of things that happened in that time, and we knew it was going to be a long season without some guys who could have helped the team if they were at a hundred percent."

Indeed, Williams's injury would not be the last suffered by a Nuggets starter in the first five weeks of the season. Shooting guard and co-captain Bryant Stith, perhaps the most competitive of all the Nuggets and a stabilizing influence in the backcourt for the rookie point guard, had undergone surgery to remove bone spurs from his right foot late the previous season. While he had gone through training camp and the exhibition season without incident, it was evident he wasn't quite right physically. The more he played, the more pain he had in his right foot. On December 4, an MRI exam revealed more bone spurs, this time in his right ankle. Another operation was required, and suddenly the Nuggets were missing 40 percent of their opening-night starting roster.

For a team whose talent level was suspect to begin with, the two injuries were a devastating blow that would send them on a downward spiral that would be dizzying before season's end. By the time New Year's Day arrived, the Nuggets had won only two of 28 games, had the worst record in the league, and were in the midst of an 11-game losing streak.

Jackson began hearing from friends—and strangers around Denver—who wanted to know what was wrong with his team. Just part of becoming a pro, Jackson figured, but hard to deal with nonetheless.

"I tried to put it behind me," he said, "come to practice, work hard every day, and leave it on the basketball court. I knew if I did that, I would have no problems outside of basketball. People are always going to recognize you and bring it up. That's the advantage and disadvantage of playing sports. If you're doing well, you get praise. If you're not doing well, people are going to talk 'mess.' I'm sorry it has come to that, but that's how it is. It's hard to deal with, especially when you're on a losing team and you've always been a winner all your life. And to jump into a situation like this, being on one of the worst teams in NBA history, we didn't want that label."

The new year began at McNichols Sports Arena against the always tough Houston Rockets. This would be the Nuggets' lone national TV game of the season, with TNT cable network doing the telecast. No Nugget wanted to be embarrassed on national TV. Whether or not that was the added motivation that made the Nuggets perform above expectations, they did. They played the Rockets to a standstill, and with 6.1 seconds left in the game, Jackson hit two free throws to give Denver a three-point lead. All the Nuggets had to do to snap their losing streak, to begin the 1998 portion of the season in fine fashion, was keep the Rockets from hitting a three-pointer that would tie the game.

Jackson had the defensive assignment on one of the Rockets' prime three-point threats, Brent Price. He lost him momentarily as Houston in-bounded the ball, and Price ended up with the ball in the corner. He fired up an off-balance desperation shot that swished through the net as regulation time expired, sending the game into overtime. To say that optimism was not exactly prevalent on the Denver bench is to understate the disappointment. There were no surprises, even though the Nuggets made it close in overtime: Houston 116, Denver 115.

"It was so frustrating," Jackson said, "when you play so hard and you know you deserve to win the game, and something like that happens in the last second and then you lose. It's frustrating, because everybody had busted his butt."

Jackson went home after the game and struggled to get to sleep, demonized by the short-term memory that his team had lost, in large part, because he had not been able to keep his man from getting off the one shot that could bury the Nuggets.

"It was unfortunate that one shot had to do us in," he said, "and obviously that was on me. It's difficult. Once a shot is hit on you, a lot of different things can take place. I tried to be strong-minded and come back in the overtime and get the win, but we didn't. And we should have won the game in regulation time."

And so the beat, and the consecutive losses, went on—13, 14, 15 . . . 21, 22, 23. The 23rd consecutive loss tied the NBA record for consecutive losses in a single season, a mark of dubious distinction established in 1994 by the Vancouver Grizzlies in their very first season as an expansion franchise.

The Nuggets arrived at the Los Angeles Sports Arena on January 24 to find additional media present, vultures waiting their chance to pick at the carrion. Just 120 miles down the road in San Diego, the Denver Broncos were putting the finishing touches on their preparations for Super Bowl XXXII, so some of the Denver media members on hand for that momentous occasion drove to Los Angeles, convinced they would see the Nuggets make dubious history. Forty-five minutes before tip-off, the players threw everyone out of their locker room— media, coaches, ball boys, trainers—and gathered in a tight circle to talk things out.

"We didn't want to be in the record books like that," Jackson said, "and that's what we talked about. Everybody had input, what we should do and shouldn't do. How we should prepare for the game."

A rookie wise beyond his years pleaded with his teammates to put everything that had happened up to that point—pouts about playing time; disagreements with the

coaches over how and when players were
used; ill feelings about hard fouls in practice; misgivings about the offensive and
defensive systems the coaches had
employed—behind them, at least for one
night.

Whether it was Jackson's urging, the players' collective pride, the position of the
moon, or simply time for The Streak to end,
the result was finally pleasant for the
Nuggets, who defeated the Clippers, 99–81.

"I'm the type of person who observes
everything but is real quiet about things that
happen," Jackson said. "The only reason I
speak up on things is if I feel I'm not being
treated well and I have a lot of anger inside
me. That's all I said, 'Come on and put
everything behind us and just play tonight,
and get this win, because we know we're better than this.' And it felt great to win, just
play our game and not have to think, after
we won, what the people were going to say,

what the media was going to say. You know the media was going to say something real negative if we set that record—that's what those guys do, and there was media from all over following us around as we were getting close to that record. And we did put everything behind us and play hard, and it felt great to win. After that game I thought maybe we should have a meeting like that before every game, because everybody came to play that night and were determined we weren't going to go in the record books with the longest losing streak."

Win number three was sweet, and the Nuggets won one of five straight home games they played leading to the annual All-Star break, doubling their win output for the season in less than a week. Jackson and teammate Danny Fortson had been selected to play in the Schick Rookie Game, part of the NBA's All-Star Weekend at Madison

Square Garden. It was a welcome respite from the grind of what had already been a nightmarish season.

Escape wasn't absolute, though. At the media interview session on Friday morning, few reporters wanted to talk to the two Denver rookies about anything but the Nuggets' struggles. Nevertheless, Jackson enjoyed the weekend, and was the Western Conference's best player on Saturday, scoring 15 points on 7-for-14 shooting, handing out seven assists and getting four steals. His team lost, however, 85–80, prompting Jackson to shrug his shoulders and say, "It doesn't matter. Wherever we go this year, we lose." Still, Jackson enjoyed two days in the Big Apple, rubbing shoulders with the game's greatest players and the celebrities who want to rub shoulders with them.

"I had the best time of my life, especially in New York," Jackson said. "No other place

could top it, with all the celebrities there
and all the great players there. I just felt
good being in that situation, where I knew I
had accomplished a lot as a rookie, and I
promised myself I wasn't going to let up,
that I would continue to work hard so that
next year, or the year after that, I could be
there again, in the real All-Star Game. It was
fun being there, and it lets you know how
hard you had worked to get there, but also
that you can't quit working."

On Saturday evening Jackson got on a
plane back to Denver, hopped in his truck at
Denver International Airport, and headed
to Wheatland, Wyoming, to spend the rest of
the weekend with his children, Breann and
Kendrick.

"I would rather have been with them the
whole weekend," he said, "but it's once in a
lifetime you get to go to All-Star Weekend
and play in the rookie game. I had a great

time, made some new friends, met some celebrities, and it was a great function for me, and for the NBA."

Through all the pain of the season up to that point, Jackson had at least been able to spend more time with Breann and Kendrick than he ever anticipated he would as an NBA player. Just three hours by car from Denver, the children had become his number-one priority. That point was driven home when he and his best friend, John Stout, headed up Interstate 25 on Christmas Eve, bound for Wheatland with a truck full of Christmas presents. Jackson had bought two battery-powered miniature cars, the kind small children can get in and drive, and they were packaged in large boxes. Only one, however, would fit in the back of Jackson's sport utility vehicle, already crammed with all the other presents, so he had to tie the other on top of the vehicle.

The weather in the Rocky Mountains in the winter seldom is predictable, and the highway between Cheyenne, Wyoming, and Wheatland is often battered by high winds. When Jackson and Stout pulled out of Denver on Christmas Eve afternoon, there was still lots of blue sky, but it had begun to get cold and dark clouds had begun to skiff across the horizon.

Not 45 minutes into the trip, the two found themselves in a wind-driven snowstorm. A few minutes later, they heard a pop. The box with the toy car atop the vehicle was being blown off the roof. Jackson pulled off I–25, and he and Stout stepped into a driving, freezing snowstorm to find the box flapping against the side of the vehicle. It would have to be retied atop the truck.

"I didn't even have a jacket on or gloves," Jackson said, "and I was freezing, and my hands were turning to ice, but I had to climb up on top of the truck and tie that car back down. John was holding the box together while I climbed on top and tied it back down, and we were both freezing to death. The trip up there usually takes about three hours, but it took us about four and a half hours. But when I got there, I didn't think anything about it when I saw my kids. For my kids, I want to do more and more, because I want them to be part of my life."

When the post-break part of the Nuggets' schedule began, there was reason to believe things might be looking up. Their first game provided a blowout win over the Boston Celtics, and Jackson easily outplayed Chauncey Billups, the Denver native who had been the first point guard drafted, the third pick overall, in Charlotte in June. It had taken the Nuggets more than a month to go from two wins to three, but only six games to go from three wins to four and then to five.

Things were looking up, but—in keeping with the season—not for long. And this time Jackson was at the center of a major distraction. He overslept and missed a practice the morning after the Boston game, and the Nuggets missed a great chance to get back-to-back wins for the first time all season when they blew a fourth-quarter lead at Sacramento. As the losses mounted, so did the frustration level of each and every Nugget. Nobody was having any fun. Tensions ran high. And on February 13, Jackson's frustrations spilled over into a heated public incident with Coach Bill Hanzlik and assistant Brian Winters.

Less than two minutes into the second half of the Nuggets' game at McNichols Arena against the Minnesota Timberwolves, Hanzlik pulled Jackson from the game after back-to-back turnovers. Jackson was extremely upset at getting yanked so quickly. Hanzlik waited on the sidelines for Jackson because he wanted to explain why he had been pulled, but Jackson brushed past him and took a seat on the bench. Winters, who is as mild-mannered a fellow as there is in the NBA, wasn't going to let Jackson get away with brushing off the head coach that way. He approached him on the bench.

But the pressure and disappointment had overwhelmed Jackson, and when that happens to rookies, the results could be volatile. No one likes to lose at any time, and the Nuggets had been embarrassed too often. Jackson took it personally, and at a time when he wanted to be left alone, Winters wanted to talk. Jackson was as inappropriate as he could be, answering Winters with a curse. The incident was featured prominently in coverage of the game in both Denver newspapers the next day, and Hanzlik would replace Jackson in the starting lineup for the Nuggets' next game at Portland.

Jackson was immediately contrite and apologized to both coaches and his teammates, but the incident would hang over his head for weeks. "Whatever I say, I'm responsible for taking the blame," he said. "It's just frustration that's built up inside you when you come out of a game early and you know you didn't do anything wrong. I know I was at fault, going off like that. I'm not one to hold my breath if I feel I haven't done anything to come out of the game. And I'll usually speak up on it. But I should have come at him in a nice manner, in a professional way, and talked to him. That's what I have to learn to do, just part of growing up. I'm taking heat for what I'm doing, and I can live with it. That's me. We talked about it, got it out of the way. I want to learn. I want to be better as a player, and I want to be better as a professional. I want to be the best player I can be in this league, and if I keep doing things like that, I don't think I will. It's going to tear me down."

Then, with the memory of the Winters incident still too fresh in everyone's minds, only nine days after helping his team beat the Celtics, Jackson broke the ring finger on his right hand, the one he uses when shooting, in a game against the Lakers and was placed on the injured list.

"It was tough," he said. "Once you know you're doing well and you think you're playing good, you get in a rhythm, and it's tough when that rhythm gets broken. When something happens that prevents you from playing, it's a shock for a while. You have to get back in shape and try to get back in the swing of things."

Jackson would miss 13 games, including the Nuggets' first back-to-back wins, on March 12 and 14, but returned to action nearly two weeks ahead of schedule, owing mostly to the hard work he did with team strength and conditioning coach Steve Hess during his rehabilitation from the fracture. Significantly, his first game back was in Charlotte on March 16, where dozens of friends and family made the short trek from his hometown of Salisbury to see him play, though his playing time was limited.

The next night, in Washington, Jackson played a very significant role in what was the team's sweetest win up to that point. The Nuggets came from behind in the fourth quarter to beat a good Washington Wizards team on its own court, and Jackson was prominent in crunch time.

"I remember Coach telling me to go in and lock up Rod [Strickland]. I came down and stole the ball from him twice in a row, and I made one three-pointer, and came down and dished it off to Danny [Fortson] for a basket, and then came through the lane for a two-pointer. So that was like seven points in less than two minutes, and then Goldy [Anthony Goldwire] hit that three-pointer to put us up by one. I have no doubt I can play this game, but I have to be focused. That game reinforced that to me after the injury. It's just that my attention span is not there all the time. For me to be successful, I have to be ready, and I have to work on that. I have to stay focused to be successful in this league. I tend to stray off at times, look up in the stands, watch the performers on the floor. But I know I can't do that, especially if I'm only going to play a certain amount of minutes."

By the time Jackson returned from his injury, he had been replaced in the starting lineup by Cory Alexander, whom the Nuggets had picked up on March 5, after the San Antonio Spurs released him. Alexander had two years of experience backing up San Antonio's fine point guard Avery Johnson, and he arrived with a fresh

supply of confidence, having been spared
the battering four months of defeats had on
the Nuggets. Alexander immediately established he could run Denver's offense and
help his teammates get good shots. Jackson,
after starting all season, found himself coming off the bench.

He didn't like it, and he liked less the fact
that his playing time began to vanish just as
the Nuggets began to get more competitive.
He played only 17 minutes of the team's
ninth win of the season, on March 27,
against Golden State, a victory that meant
the Nuggets could not finish with the worst
record in NBA history. The win over the
Warriors meant they could merely share
that dubious distinction with the 1972–73
Philadelphia 76ers. Then, on the night the
Nuggets finally got the 10th win that would
remove them from the crosshairs of NBA
infamy, Jackson had one of his worst nights
of the season.

He had been in a shooting slump, having missed 19-of-22 shots in the previous three games, and Hanzlik decided to make Stith, back on the bench after recovering from his latest operation, the first guard off the bench instead of Jackson. In the final minutes of a blowout win over the Sacramento Kings that had the crowd at McNichols Arena on its feet and dancing in celebration, Hanzlik finally called on Jackson to go into the game, with only 1:32 remaining. Jackson walked toward the scorer's table to report, but when he reached the spot where Hanzlik was standing, Jackson didn't move. He cursed at his coach. "Hey," Hanzlik retorted, "do you get paid to play the game?"

Jackson just stared back at him, and Hanzlik sent him back to take a seat on the bench. It was a lamentable moment in a discouraging season, and it spoiled the celebration for both coach and player. The next day, the Nuggets would fine Jackson for his insubordination, and he agreed to apologize to his teammates for his actions. It was the second instance of anger overtaking the rookie's common sense, and Jackson tossed and turned that night as he tried to reconcile his actions to himself.

"The thing with Coach Hanzlik is something I have got to live with," he said. "I'm willing to take responsibility for what I've done. I know I was in the wrong, but everybody's not perfect. I hope people don't judge me based on the two incidents that happened. I'm a real nice guy if you get to know me. I'm down to earth. But things happen and there could have been ways to resolve them better, but it was just stupidity on my part. I wasn't really thinking at the time. I just wasn't thinking. I was frustrated because I didn't get in the game at all. Some things happen. Me and Coach talked about it, and it's something I need to work on. I'm the one at fault. But you can't be a starter, and then not play until the fourth quarter. I'd been playing 30, 35 minutes a game. I felt that was an insult to me.

"I'm happy we won. I know it's not all about me being jealous, but it's about me being treated fairly. I work extremely hard, just like the other guys, and to be put in a situation like that, where you're not going to play until the last minute and 30 seconds, it was totally an insult to me. If I feel like I'm not being treated equally, I'm going to speak up on it, but I need to choose better when and where I speak. If I had to do it again, I would have gone in the game, and then talked to Coach after the game. Hindsight's 20–20."

Although only a rookie, Jackson was experienced enough to know what the public's reaction would be. And he knew that his actions would negate so many of the positives that he had accomplished.

"People didn't expect me to do all the good things I've done this season. But now I've had these two incidents with my coaches, and they're probably calling me a knucklehead. I am not a knucklehead. There are just some things that happened. You learn from your mistakes. Everybody's not perfect. Even though we're making a lot of money, everybody has reason to do and say things sometimes, but they should never be out in public, like I've done, and I regret doing that. I had to get my word across, but I regret how I did it, how things happened."

When the Nuggets ended their season with a loss at the Alamodome to the same Spurs team that they had opened the season against, Jackson stared across the arena at Duncan, who soon would be named Rookie of the Year after one of the most successful rookie seasons in NBA history. He could not

help but think about the disparate roads the
two had traveled since that night on the
final day of October when their seasons had
begun with such promise. And he could not
help but think of how it was supposed to be
different. Duncan was so lucky that circumstances allowed him—the number-one
player in the draft—to play with a great
team led by David Robinson. If the draft
had worked in a traditional manner,
Duncan would have been a great player on
a bad team while Jackson—the 23rd player
taken in the draft—would have played with
a good team. Jackson imagined himself in
Seattle, backing up Gary Payton, playing
with a team that won 61 games and was playoff bound. Instead, he would watch
Duncan.

"His game has gone dramatically up, and
mine has gone dramatically down," Jackson
said, "probably because of injuries. The
team situation has a lot to do with it, too,

but it shouldn't be that way. If you just go out and play hard, work on your game, you can't help but do better. The Lord is going to take care of you. If He knows you're working hard, and knows you're trying hard, you can't ask for anything more. You go through things for a reason. I'm not mad I'm in the situation I'm in. I'm happy to be in this league. But Tim is one of the rare players who can come out as a rookie and do what he has done. He's one of the very best players in the league. I have got a lot of things to work on, but people didn't give me much of a chance to even be in this league. That's the difference between Tim and me. Everybody expected him to be a good player in this league. He was the first pick in our class; I was the 23rd pick."

He didn't say it, but he didn't have to: Duncan's team won 56 games and headed off to the playoffs; Jackson's team won 11 games, and barely escaped the worst record

in league history. The day after the season
finale, Jackson got another reminder of the
harsh reality of NBA life. Hanzlik was fired
by new General Manager Dan Issel,
Hanzlik's good friend and former teammate who had been hired less than a month
earlier to direct a turnaround of the moribund franchise. In his heart of hearts,
Jackson knew he had contributed significantly to Hanzlik's dismissal by throwing his
two celebrated tantrums. He felt bad
Hanzlik had become the first fall guy for the
Nuggets' horrendous season.

"Every coach has his own coaching ways,"
Jackson said. "He wasn't a discipline guy. He
was a nice guy, a players' coach. He's a guy
you would love to have on your staff because
he gets along with everybody. It's not his fault.
It's the players' fault that we put him in that
situation. Bill gave me a chance to play. I can
just thank him for that. We had our differ-
ences. We fought, but we put it behind us."

With that, Jackson cleaned out his locker at McNichols Arena and headed up the highway to Wheatland. Breann and Kendrick were waiting there to see their daddy, who viewed the NBA with a wiser, more seasoned eye.

Daddy wasn't a rookie anymore.

eight
The Rookie of the Year

It was inevitable that Tim Duncan's entire rookie season would be linked with that of his teammate, 1995 NBA Most Valuable Player David Robinson. The two shared so much, from their physical attributes and skills to their temperaments and level of local and national expectation. Never mind that Robinson was a veteran of eight years, a member of three Olympic teams—including the legendary original Dream Team, and a winner of one Most Valuable Player award. It did not matter. Robinson would be the standard, and Duncan had to measure up. At least that was the way it was at the beginning of the season.

Robinson had come to the Spurs in 1989 with the same great expectations Duncan faced in the 1997–98 season. The number-one pick in the 1987 Draft, he had first served in the United States Navy for 18 months before being released from active duty because he was too tall to serve on a ship. When he finally joined the Spurs in 1989, they were coming off a horrid season, and he was expected to lead them back to the NBA's elite level.

When Duncan arrived, the number-one pick in the 1997 NBA Draft, he had just as heavy a burden, tempered significantly, however, by the fact he would have Robinson around to help in the resuscitation of a moribund team.

It was natural, then, for Duncan to gravitate to Robinson as a role model, mentor, and friend, and the two began bonding even before the Spurs went to training camp for Duncan's first season. Robinson invited Duncan to join him in his preseason workouts at his summer home in Aspen, Colorado, in the rarefied air of the Rocky Mountains. Robinson has a vigorous regimen that has made him one of pro basketball's best-conditioned big men.

Duncan leaped at the chance. Having just completed the Rocky Mountain Revue in Salt Lake City, the summer tournament for NBA rookies and free agents, he discovered that his skills were where they needed to be to play in the NBA, but his conditioning wasn't. To be allowed to work on his conditioning and strength with a teammate who obviously knew what it would take to be ready for the new level of competition was an opportunity Duncan did not want to waste. Immediately, Robinson discovered a kindred spirit.

"Our personalities are so similar,"

Robinson said. "It's like he's where I was 10 years ago. He came in and he had a great attitude. When we went out and worked out, he never complained, and I dragged him through the mud a little bit. I made him work. I didn't lighten up my workouts for him, even though I knew he just came off a week in Utah. I figured he was in pretty good shape. So I worked him pretty hard, and he never complained. He came out and he showed a great attitude. I love being around him. He impressed me then by how hard he worked. I'll tell you, I never worked that hard as a rookie."

After Duncan worked out for a couple of weeks with Robinson, he returned to San Antonio. Many of Duncan's new teammates began showing up there as well, and daily pickup games were informally scheduled at a local gym. Robinson, still recovering from the back and leg injuries that had shelved him for all but six games the previous season, soon discovered the unpolished gem the Spurs had mined in the draft.

"We would play in the pickup games," Robinson said, "and he was scoring on me left and right, and I'm thinking, 'Gol-lee, this boy is pretty good on the block, and he can shoot the ball. Here's some real competition for me.' Even though he's a teammate and you want him to do well, I'm out here playing pickup games and he's making me look bad. Part of that is making each other better, and part of it is understanding each other better."

Training camp did nothing to make anyone in the Spurs family, especially Robinson, believe Duncan was not capable of having one of the best rookie seasons in NBA history. Still, Duncan wrestled with the demons of self-doubt.

"I used to wake up at 4 A.M. going, 'Oh, my God, am I good enough to play with these guys?'" he said.

His answer would come quickly, during the Spurs' first few exhibition games. But first Duncan would be subjected to a prank that has been pulled on NBA rookies for decades. Nearly every rookie who ever has come into the NBA has been put through the relatively harmless but nonetheless humiliating first-game ritual that goes like this: The rookie is told, matter-of-factly, that when the teams jog out for pregame warm-ups, the rookies get at the head of the line and jog out first. Then, when the rookie begins to trot onto the court for the layup line, the veterans stop after a few steps and let their unknowing first-year teammate run on the court all alone, left to look around in confusion while the paying customers laugh.

Duncan may have been the number-one pick in the draft, but he was still a rookie, so team co-captain Avery Johnson explained the rookies-first custom as the Spurs readied for their pregame trot-out in their exhibition home opener at the Alamodome. Sure enough, Duncan jogged out, only to look back to see his teammates, doubled over in laughter at a teammate they believed they had duped.

But there was a catch. Duncan had known precisely what the veterans had planned for him, but went along with the joke anyway.

"I knew what they were going to do," he said. "But I went out anyway. It was just for fun. I'm a rookie."

A rookie? True, but Duncan hardly played like a neophyte, which perhaps shouldn't have been surprising considering that Duncan was a "typical" NBA rookie in name only. Yes, he entered the NBA in the same year as Tracy McGrady, but because Duncan had stayed in college, he had four more years of experience than McGrady. It showed. In an exhibition against the Houston Rockets, one of the Spurs' Midwest

Division rivals and a team expected to contend for the Western Conference title, Duncan scored 17 points and grabbed 17 rebounds. That prompted Houston forward Charles Barkley, one of the NBA's 50 Greatest Players and an astute observer of the game known both for his rapier wit and refreshing honesty, to gush: "I have seen the future, and he wears number 21. He was quite impressive, better than I expected, and I was expecting a lot. He's polished. Very polished."

Duncan averaged 18 points and 10.4 rebounds in the preseason and was clearly ready for the regular season to begin. On opening night, he found himself at McNichols Sports Arena in Denver, nervous but nonetheless ready to begin his pro career against a rebuilding team that had four rookies on the opening night roster, including a point guard named Bobby Jackson who had waited for 22 picks after

Duncan's selection on draft night before hearing his name called in the first round.

By game's end, Duncan had logged 35 minutes, made six of nine shots, three of five free throws, grabbed 10 rebounds, and scored 15 points.

His rookie thunder, however, had been stolen by Jackson, who scored 27 points and sparked a Denver rally in the fourth quarter.

Duncan, though, emerged with what was most important: a victory in his very first game, Spurs' 107–96 win. Robinson scored 21 points and grabbed 13 rebounds, and was the focus of San Antonio's offense in the fourth quarter when the Spurs blunted Denver's rally.

Through the first month of the season, Duncan played no fewer than 22 minutes in any of the Spurs' 16 games, and his statistics already were beginning to shout "greatness" to anyone paying attention. His first 20-point game came in his seventh game as a pro, a 22-point performance at Minnesota in a game that put the Spurs at 6–1 for the season. Robinson secured the 93–92 victory with a tip at the buzzer.

Two nights later at Chicago's United Center, the rookie went up against the Bulls' relentless rebounder, Dennis Rodman, and came away with 22 rebounds, which would be his season-high and also would open a lot of eyes in the home of the two-time defending NBA champions, even though the Spurs lost in double overtime.

"I can see why he went number one," said Bulls superstar Michael Jordan, duly impressed. "He has a lot of talent. He's matured. He's blossomed. He stayed those four years in college, and his dividend is starting to show."

Because of the Spurs' 6–1 start—but also because of the hype surrounding him— much more was expected of Duncan than was reasonable of any rookie. When the

Spurs struggled through the final two weeks of November, losing six of nine games, a few harsh critics began to wonder aloud if Duncan was as good as advertised.

The moment Duncan landed on a team whose number-one draft position resulted from misfortune rather than lack of talent, the Spurs became a contender for the 1998 NBA title. With Robinson recovered from the back woes, the addition of the gifted 7–0 Duncan, fairly or unfairly, put the Spurs in company with the Bulls, Jazz, Lakers, Sonics, Heat, Knicks, and Rockets.

Conversely, when the Spurs struggled, Duncan got much of the blame. Spurs Coach Gregg Popovich, though, had a firm grip on the reins of outrageous expectation.

"I think people's expectations for new people coming into the league are always a little ridiculous," Popovich said in early December. "They get overly excited about everybody and expect them to be either

Magic Johnson or Kareem. With Tim Duncan I think you have those kinds of expectations because you see the amazing skill level he has. He can play outside; he can play inside; he can pass, catch, shoot, dribble . . . everything. He's got it all. So it's going to make those expectations high. I think, at the start of the season, he lived up to them. Then it got difficult for him, basically because our perimeter game went on vacation.

"What people have done is take Tim Duncan and David out of the game, and said, 'Your other guys are going to have to beat us.' And we've been just atrocious—God-awful, a nightmare, a horror show—from the perimeter. So Tim has been in a really tough spot and not able to contribute that much offensively because of that. And it's going to stay like that until we start making some shots."

The Spurs' shooters began to make their

shots again, and Duncan's rapid development as a pro was reignited. Through the
first six weeks of the season, Duncan showed
not only that he had the skills to be one of
the best big men in the game, but the basketball intelligence only the truly great players have, an innate court sense that sepa-
rates mere All-Stars from future Hall of
Famers. Take the Spurs' November 29 game
against the Dallas Mavericks, for example.
Two plays demonstrated court savvy surpass-
ing even that of veteran players:

In the first quarter, Robinson got caught
on a defensive switch that left his man
unguarded on the baseline. Duncan had to
cover Robinson's man, but instead of running to him immediately, he hung back, in
traffic, waiting until Maverick guard Erick
Strickland attempted a pass he easily picked
off. Did Duncan know the pass was coming
and lure Strickland into throwing it?

"I'm not that good," Duncan said, laughing. "I don't know if I had a sense of what was going to happen, but I knew there was an opportunity the ball would go there, and I was the next available man, so I just...."

So he just made a play few other players would have. Later, Dallas guard Khalid Reeves knocked the ball out of Duncan's hands in the post and took off for the opposite end ahead of everyone. Duncan trailed Reeves downcourt, and when Reeves laid the ball in, Duncan snatched it out of the net, jumped out of bounds, and fired a baseball pass to teammate Avery Johnson in the Spurs' frontcourt. Suddenly, San Antonio had a four-on-two that produced an easy basket.

"Well," Duncan said, "I was thinking, 'Look up the floor because he [Reeves] is down here, so somebody's got to be up the floor.'"

"You just don't expect that from a rookie," said Johnson. "You expect something like that from a real smart veteran."

Someone like Larry Bird, Avery?

"Well . . . yeah," Johnson said.

When Bird retired in 1992, Duncan was 16, and had been playing basketball only three years. The fact that Duncan came to the game late—he was a competitive swimmer in his native Virgin Islands until age 12 when Hurricane Hugo ravaged St. Croix and destroyed the pool where he had trained—made his cerebral approach to the game even more amazing.

"I don't know that I understand the game better than most players," Duncan said. "I wouldn't put down other people like that. But I do think I have a good understanding of the game. I'm not as athletic as some of the guys out there, not as strong as some of the guys. I have to find a way to fit in. By knowing basketball, knowing how to use what I have, it makes me more effective."

Some of the things Duncan seemed to

know about the game can't be taught.

"There are a lot of people who are good players," Spurs assistant coach Hank Egan said, "both offensively and defensively—a lot of people with good skills. I don't think there are a whole lot of people who really understand this game. It's a pretty complicated thing, this game. It's played on the fly, and a lot of decisions have to be made on the fly. A lot of it you've just got to have a feel, and Tim has that. He can pass the ball; he knows when to give the guy room; he knows when a guy needs help; he knows where to go to get a rebound. I don't think you can coach those things. They come by feel."

Duncan recorded the first 30-point game of his career on December 13, against Orlando, beginning a stretch of 14 games when he would average exactly 20 points and 11.9 rebounds. Those were All-Star numbers, and by the time the 1998 portion of the 1997–98 season arrived, it was evident to nearly everyone Duncan was not merely the best rookie in the league; he was one of its best players, deserving of All-Star status.

In late January, the NBA announced the players selected for the 1998 NBA All-Star Game, to be played at New York's Madison Square Garden. Though his teammates and the San Antonio media had been insisting for weeks Duncan deserved to be on the team, Duncan's goal had remained merely to play in the annual Schick Rookie Game on All-Star Saturday.

On the morning of January 22, Popovich summoned him to his office before a Spurs practice. Duncan wondered what he had done wrong to get called in for a talk with the coaching staff. When he got there, Popovich told him he had been selected to the Western Conference All-Star team.

"My coaches called me to the office and just threw it on me," Duncan said, "like,

'Oh, yeah, by the way, you made the All-Star team.' It was like being called to the principal's office, wondering what you did wrong, and being told you made the honor roll."

Once the shock of his selection wore off, Duncan began to realize the significance of the honor that had been bestowed on him. When he met the San Antonio media after practice to answer questions about his selection, he was typically humble.

"It's great," he said. "I really can't do it justice now because I just learned about it a couple of hours ago. I didn't think I would make it. David [Robinson] congratulated me and said I deserved to be on the team."

Making the All-Star team as a rookie had never been a goal?

"No way did I think that when I came into the league," Duncan said. "I just wanted to play well enough to make sure I didn't get left off the rookie team."

The occasion gave him a chance to evaluate the first half of his rookie season.

"It has met every expectation and exceeded them," he said. "There are a lot of games I can feel myself getting tired, getting beat up in there."

When All-Star Weekend arrived on February 5, Duncan and Robinson flew together to New York for an entire weekend of festivities. Friday morning was given over to a round of media interviews, each player assigned a table in a ballroom of a midtown Manhattan hotel to meet the press. Duncan is not particularly comfortable in dealing with the media, but he had no choice. He found himself surrounded by reporters and cameramen, all wielding notepads, mini-cams, tape recorders, or microphones. Patiently, he answered question after question, often the same one, over and over.

Did he think he would reach All-Star status so quickly?

"I was trying to, of course," Duncan

would answer. "I thought it would be a great honor, but I didn't really expect it. I never considered it a goal to make it; it was more like a dream. I am happy to be here."

And on and on and on.

His All-Star Game experience would be minimal, although he did have an impact. He played only 14 minutes, scored only two points, but he grabbed 11 rebounds, which tied Shawn Kemp and Eddie Jones, both of whom played more minutes than Duncan. Duncan fans were left to wonder: What if he had played 25 or 30 minutes?

Back in San Antonio after the break, Duncan and his teammates would resume their quest to qualify for the 1998 NBA Playoffs in one of the top four spots in the Western Conference, assuring them home-court advantage at least through the first round.

Duncan's transition to the pros had been

eased by the nature of the Spurs team. Led by Robinson and Johnson, both devout Christians who had engendered a family atmosphere on the team for several years, the Spurs seemed more to Duncan like a college team than a pro team. It was easy fitting in.

"We are a close-knit group," Duncan said. "Everybody is like family around here, so it's no big deal. I've heard horror stories about some teams, and some sets of players. I think it's just a blessing to have a group of guys like this, and sometimes surprising. But going through college, and all the teams I've been on, it's been similar to this, so it seems like the norm to me. It's a lot like the four years I went through in college. It makes it a lot easier to deal with people, to handle people. You can joke with them, and they're going to be right there to help you out."

Johnson, the Spurs' vocal leader, knew

Duncan would fit right in on a team with "family values."

"I think, over the years, chemistry has been a big part of our ballclub," Johnson said. "We take care of each other—one day last week I was sick and Vinny [Del Negro] brought me some food by the house, or we go to Sean Elliott's house, eight or nine guys, maybe watching a fight on TV or something—and for Tim coming into a situation where you have a ballclub that's really close, you don't have any ego problems. You don't have guys talking about contracts every game; you just let those things take care of themselves. That's an easy transition for a first-year player.

"We stay together. We haven't had guys going separate ways this year. As you've seen in years past, we've had some good teams, but we've always had one or two guys who had different agendas, who tried to take away from the team, but this year we've had everybody on the same page. Tim was a big part of that when he came in, and I think that's what really has enabled us to get to this point we're at now."

In mid-February, Robinson missed six straight games with chondromalacia—jumper's knee—of the right knee. By then, more comfortable with the pro game and his role on the Spurs, Duncan took up the slack and led the Spurs in scoring in each of the games Robinson missed. In fact, in a 12-game stretch from February 3 through March 4, he was San Antonio's top scorer in every game, including a March game at Golden State where he scored a season-high 35 points and grabbed 17 rebounds—his third consecutive 17-rebound game. And Robinson was back in the lineup for the last three of those games.

Naturally, Spurs observers began to muse about the relative merits of the Spurs' two great big men, and something of a mild controversy began to brew over which of the 7-footers was the team's most valuable.

Duncan was uncomfortable with such comparisons, but he did nothing to dispel such talk when he played three spectacular games in the final two weeks of the season after Robinson suffered a concussion when Utah's Karl Malone inadvertently elbowed him in the head in April, sending him to a Salt Lake City hospital.

Duncan scored 28, 26, and 32 points in the three games Robinson missed, which included a win over Pacific Division power Seattle two nights after Robinson's injury, and he pulled down 17, 16, and 10 rebounds.

Robinson returned for the April 17 game at Seattle, but it was Duncan who led the Spurs to an important 89–87 win, scoring 31 and grabbing eight boards.

When Duncan's first playoffs rolled around—the Spurs would have to start on the road against the Phoenix Suns, who edged them for the fourth spot in the final Western Conference standings—he entered them as a full-fledged NBA star. He soon discovered that he would be his team's "go-to" guy when playoff games were on the line.

In his first NBA postseason game at Phoenix's America West Arena, Duncan performed like a playoff-savvy veteran, especially when the game hit crunch time. He scored 28 of his game-high 32 points in the second half, but more amazing was a run in the fourth quarter. With the outcome very much in question, he seared the nets for 12 consecutive Spurs points and finished with 18 points in the final period.

The "Who's the Man?" question raged in San Antonio, and it seemed that many fans and even some members of the media had fallen into the trap of wanting to choose between teammates. Others wondered, "Why choose when you have two great players?"

Say that Duncan does become the Man. Is that a reason to trade Robinson? Are the Spurs not better off with two 7-foot-tall franchise players rather than one 7-footer and a couple of guards, no matter how good they are? There's an old NBA saying that goes: Never trade big for little.

"At times during his career, there has been some disappointment with Robinson's perceived lack of aggressiveness," said *San Antonio Express-News* columnist Buck Harvey. "But there has been too much concern about what he can't do. I think everyone should concentrate on what he can do. He's one of the best defensive players in the league, and that will help Duncan tremendously because Duncan won't have to worry about defense as much. It's obvious that the Spurs can't trade Robinson for a Michael Jordan. Any step down from that level makes it not worth it."

But in San Antonio the issue had been

created, and the debate began. Duncan, of
course, was reluctant to snatch the mantle
of leadership from around the shoulders of
Robinson, his friend and teammate.
Robinson was reluctant to give it up. But
Duncan knew the playoffs were no time to
defer to anyone, and so did Robinson.

Still, the passing of the torch of greatness
on one of the NBA's most competitive
teams became an awkward subplot during a
playoff run that would both excite Spurs
fans and ultimately disappoint them.

The Suns, burned so badly when they
didn't double-team the rookie in Game 1,
dramatically altered their defensive tactics
in Game 2. Every time Duncan touched the
ball, the Suns, using a small lineup that
sometimes featured four guards on the
floor, ran at the rookie with extra defenders,
sometimes one, more often two. By game's
end, Duncan and the Spurs were totally
frustrated in a 108–101 loss. Duncan made

only six of 11 shots and turned the ball over three times. He and Robinson, fouled early and often, combined to make only 16 of 30 free throws. Still, the Spurs had managed to steal home-court advantage in the best-of-five series with a Game 1 victory, returning to the relative safety of the Alamodome knowing they could close out the series with two home wins.

Before they arrived back in San Antonio, NBA officials had informed the Spurs that Duncan was a landslide winner of the 1997–98 Schick Rookie of the Year Award. A ceremony was scheduled for the morning before Game 3, with a shorter presentation to take place just before tipoff of that night's game.

Although it was hardly surprising that he had received the award, the results of the voting caused shock waves throughout the NBA and among fans all over the world. Duncan had received 113 of 116 votes, with the other three going to New Jersey's Keith Van Horn.

No one could understand how Duncan, who had won the NBA Rookie of the Month award every month of the regular season, was not the unanimous choice. It was nothing negative toward Van Horn. But compare the two lines:

- Duncan played 82 games while Van Horn missed 20 because of injury.
- Duncan made 55 percent of his field goals while Van Horn made 43 percent.
- Duncan averaged 21.1 points while Van Horn averaged 19.7.
- Duncan averaged 11.9 rebounds while Van Horn averaged 6.6.
- And the Spurs won 56 games to the Nets' 43.

While a healthy Van Horn possibly would have challenged Duncan for rookie honors, the fact is that Van Horn missed nearly one-fourth of the season. How could a player who played 75 percent of the time be better than Tim Duncan?

Duncan, of course, cared even less about that debate than he did about the "Who's the Man?" foolishness. When he arrived at the presentation ceremony to receive the Eddie Gottlieb Rookie of the Year trophy, he was typically humble and nonchalant. His first question was: "Do I give a speech or something?"

Informed he was indeed expected to say a few words to the assembled media and representatives of Schick, the award's sponsor, he gave the shortest acceptance speech in the history of the award.

"I'd like to thank my teammates and coaching staff," he said, "and everyone who kept me sane this year."

That was it, though he did answer a few more questions put to him by reporters.

"I was fortunate," he said, "because I didn't have to come in and save the team. There were great players who were already here. All I had to do was fit in and learn my way."

Was he offended he hadn't been a unanimous winner?

"Keith had a great year," he said. "He played through a lot of injuries. It might have been different if he had been healthy."

Others, though, knew it was a travesty that he had not been a unanimous pick.

"He's the best rookie I've ever seen," then-Seattle Coach George Karl said. "I think back and, yes, I would say he's the best. He's a quiet assassin, skilled in all aspects of the game."

It was an amazing tribute from one of the NBA's most competitive coaches, but Duncan went out that very night and proved Karl was correct. In a 100–88 Game

3 win over the Suns, Duncan made 11 of 21 shots and grabbed 14 rebounds, again the focus of the Spurs' offense in the fourth quarter. The next day, after a practice session at the Alamodome, reporters from around the country descended on the Spurs and again demanded to know if Duncan had supplanted Robinson as San Antonio's most important player.

Duncan did his best to deflect the notion, but Robinson addressed it forthrightly. Just three years removed from recognition as the Most Valuable Player in the NBA, Robinson was waltzing with the perception that he no longer was the MVP of his own team. One of the best big men in league history patiently met with the press at the Alamodome and talked and talked . . . and talked some more . . . about Tim Duncan.

When Duncan finished with an impromptu photo shoot after the practice session, he took his own spot on the sidelines for his round of interviews, and all the mini-cams and microphones bade a hasty, somewhat rude good-bye to Robinson and rushed to hear what the new hero of the Alamo had to say. Robinson did his best to keep a smile on his face as he witnessed the exodus, and he shrugged his shoulders. Finally, a reporter asked him the question others had tiptoed around all morning.

"After watching Duncan score 12 straight points in the fourth quarter of the Spurs' Game 1 win over the Phoenix Suns, did you say to yourself that Duncan had become 'the man' on this team, David?"

And Robinson laughed.

"No, I don't say that," he said, "not at all. My thing is: Whatever it takes to make this team better, that's what we've got to do. You've got to put your ego aside. I don't care. If we're better with him scoring down the stretch, I have no problem with that at all. If we get the win, I go home with a smile on my face. The thing is, I know there are still a lot of things I have to do for this team, whether it's to put the ball in the basket, or find open guys, or block shots and protect the basket. I have to do those things, and I set that tone. That's my leadership, from the beginning of the game to the end of the game, and guys know that. So I don't look at it that way.

"Everybody talks about this shifting thing," Robinson continued, "but he's still just learning, and he's got a lot of great stuff, but he's still got a ways to go before you can say he's in that Hakeem [Olajuwon] category. It's just taking time. But I don't have a problem. If he gets to that point and he's making shots like Hakeem, then, shoot, I'll be a role player and make this team better defensively."

Robinson's and Duncan's teammates were acutely aware of the changing of the

guard that was taking place before their
eyes, protective of their longtime teammate
and co-captain but realistic enough to
understand the reality that Robinson himself understood.

"Most great teams have two superstars,"
Avery Johnson, Robinson's best buddy
among the Spurs, said. "We have had one
for quite a while. The rest of us are role
players, and if we haven't figured that out,
we're in trouble. We needed another guy
like Tim Duncan. Dave welcomed that,
just like Michael [Jordan] welcomed
Scottie [Pippen] and Hakeem welcomed
Clyde Drexler. I'm talking about two
superstars, and that gives us a better
chance. We joke about it in the locker
room, but I'm glad to be talking about
Tim Duncan. Last year I was somewhere in
Jamaica this time of year. I'd rather be
going to the Finals every year, just to have

a shot at it, just to see that NBA logo on the floor. I'm glad. I'm glad he's on my team, yes, indeed."

The Spurs rolled to a clinching win in Game 4 of the series, crushing the Suns 99–80. Duncan and Robinson both deferred to Johnson, charitably listed at six feet on the Spurs' roster. The "Little General" scored 30 points, Robinson 15, Duncan only 11. The Spurs could win a big game with someone other than Duncan making the key shots, it turned out.

Beating Phoenix put the Spurs in a Western Conference semifinal series against defending Western champion Utah. The Jazz had earned home-court advantage throughout the playoffs after a 62–20 season that included two wins over the defending NBA champion Chicago Bulls. Advancing to the Western Conference Finals was going to require at least one win in Utah's Delta Center, which is a sonic torture chamber for visiting teams, never more than in the playoffs.

And when the Spurs took the floor for Game 1, they seemed intimidated by their surroundings, falling behind by 16, the Jazz fans howling in approval. Popovich gathered his troops during a timeout in the second period and blitzed them, launching a profanity-filled tirade that would either inspire or bring his team down.

The Spurs chose inspiration. They rallied and got back in the game, and in the fourth quarter it appeared they might pull a duplication of their Game 1 win in the Phoenix series. Going to Duncan nearly every time down the floor, the Spurs got within one point with 4.1 seconds left. They had the ball and a timeout to set up a play that could have won the game and stolen home-court advantage. Everyone in the arena knew who the ball would be going to: Duncan, who already had 17 points in the period, missing only one of his eight shots.

Duncan got the ball on the right side of the court, 17 feet from the basket. He made a small fake against defender Greg Foster, then launched a jumper that appeared to be right on line to go in. Instead, it bounced off the back of the rim, sealing Utah's 83–82 victory and crushing San Antonio's hopes.

When the buzzer sounded to end the game, as the ball bounced harmlessly off the rim, Popovich rushed to midcourt to meet his young star. He told Duncan to forget about the miss, that there would be many more opportunities to make game-winning shots.

"I had to go over there and tell him, 'Hey, you missed a shot, it's not the end of the world,'" Popovich explained. "'You played a great game and you're going to have a whole lot more of those in your career. Some are going to go in; some aren't. Hell with it. Tomorrow morning you go back to work.' Then he's fine. It's the right reaction. You question yourself. Coaches do it. Players do it. Then the next day you go back to work."

Again, it had become crystal clear Duncan was his team's go-to guy, a rookie burdened with the responsibility of great- ness and leadership. The next day Popovich discussed Duncan's willingness to take shots like the one he missed the previous night.

"Tim's a special player," Popovich said. "Everybody has figured that out by now, that he's somebody who needs to get touches out there on the floor. He doesn't care if it's regular season, playoffs, off-season. When he steps on the court, he just comes to play. Being a rookie passed him a long time ago."

Duncan didn't want to talk about the missed shot, but he had no choice.

"I have no problem with it," he said. "I had a good look at the basket. I wish it went down, but it didn't. It's not going to change anything. That's a shot I take, and if I have that shot tomorrow, I'll take it again. When I think about it now, I wish I had put it on the floor, one or two [dribbles], taken a little more time. But I saw it on the replay, and I had a good look at it, and I thought that as the ball came out, but it just didn't go down for me."

In Game 2 the Spurs led most of the game before the Jazz rallied and tied the score, this time with 2.3 seconds left.

Timeout, San Antonio.

Just as they had in Game 1, the Spurs had a chance to win the game with a last-second shot. And just like the previous night, it was Duncan for whom the play was called. This time, though, he got the ball with his back to the basket. With little opportunity to turn and shoot before time expired, he spotted teammate Jaren Jackson, wide open in the left corner, and flicked a pass to him. Jackson's shot from three-point range missed, and the game went into overtime.

The Jazz prevailed, 109–106.

More than being down 0–2, the Spurs knew they were in serious trouble because Duncan had suffered a sprained left ankle in the fourth quarter. After an injury-free season, Duncan faced physical misfortune, just when he and the Spurs could least afford it. The rest of the series was almost an afterthought. Yes, the Spurs won Game 3 on their Alamodome court, but Duncan quietly was struggling with his injury, hardly at full strength.

Utah won Game 4, and on the flight back to Salt Lake City for Game 5, Duncan's ankle swelled badly, an apparent reaction to the difference in air pressure during the flight. In Game 5 he was a shadow of his rookie-season self, and the Jazz won easily.

By game's end, a look of utter dejection

had clouded Duncan's face, so stark TV commentators felt compelled to point it out. It was a disappointing end to one of the greatest rookie seasons in NBA history. But Duncan would realize in the days that followed the Game 5 disappointment that his future in San Antonio was secure and exciting.

Just eight days after exiting the playoffs, Duncan was named to the All-NBA First Team—the first rookie since Larry Bird in 1980—taking his place alongside such luminaries as Jordan, Karl Malone, Shaquille O'Neal, and Gary Payton. He had joined the big leagues at the beginning of the season, wondering if he was good enough to play with "these guys." At the end, he would become one of those guys.

He enters the 1998–99 season no longer a rookie, and the expectations are certain to be greater. But after a season when he swept all the rookie awards and joined an elite club as one of the NBA's five best players, can anyone in his right mind expect even more? The answer is yes. It's a fact of life in the NBA that once the bar has been raised, it stays high and the only direction it's allowed to go is up. That's why Robinson has to answer questions about his seemingly declining role on the team. That, too, will someday be Duncan's fate, but not now.

"Man, it's ridiculous how good Tim is," Popovich said. "He can shoot the jumper. He's got range to the three-point line. He's got jump hooks right and left. He can catch it, pull it through, and drive it on people. He can drive it and pull up for the jumper. On defense, he runs back as well as anybody. He can guard a big forward or small forward. Then he can get inside and guard a center. He's a shot blocker. He's incredible. Tim Duncan just wants to get better. He's not impressed with the hype."

Duncan, as always, was humbled by the praise.

"It's a great feeling when you hear something like that," said Duncan, the man who began playing basketball because Hugo the hurricane destroyed a swimming pool. "Of course I am flattered, but I know I have a lot of work to do and a long way to go. So I take the compliments, say thanks, and then let them go. I still have a lot to prove. I've come a long way playing this game. I'm very fortunate to be where I am today. Who knows? Without Hugo, I might still be swimming."

ROOKIE
LEADERS
STATISTICS

FINAL 1997–1998 ROOKIE STATISTICS

SCORING AVERAGE	G	FG	FT	PTS	AVG
Duncan, S.A.	**82**	**706**	**319**	**1731**	**21.1**
Van Horn, N.J.	**62**	**446**	**258**	**1219**	**19.7**
Mercer, Bos.	80	515	188	1221	15.3
Ilgauskas, Cle.	82	454	230	1139	13.9
Anderson, Cle.	66	239	275	770	11.7
Jackson, Den.	**68**	**310**	**149**	**790**	**11.6**
Taylor, LA-C	71	321	173	815	11.5
Billups, Bos.-Tor.	80	280	226	893	11.2
Thomas, Phi.	77	306	171	845	11.0
Fortson, Den.	80	276	263	816	10.2
Henderson, Cle.	82	348	136	832	10.1
Funderburke, Sac.	52	191	110	493	9.5
Knight, Cle.	80	261	201	723	9.0
Battie, Den.	65	234	73	544	8.4
Daniels, Van.	74	228	112	579	7.8
Washington, Den.	66	201	65	511	7.7
Johnson, Sac.	77	226	80	574	7.5
McGrady, Tor.	**64**	**179**	**79**	**451**	**7.0**
Honeycutt, Mil.	38	90	36	245	6.4
Abdul-Wahad, Sac.	59	144	84	376	6.4

FINAL 1997–1998 ROOKIE STATISTICS

REBOUNDS PER GAME	G	OFF	DEF	TOT	AVG
Duncan, S.A.	**82**	**274**	**703**	**977**	**11.9**
Ilgauskas, Cle.	82	279	444	723	8.8
Stewart, Sac.	81	197	339	536	6.6
Van Horn, N.J.	**62**	**142**	**266**	**408**	**6.6**
Fortson, Den.	80	182	266	448	5.6
Battie, Den.	65	138	213	351	5.4
Funderburke, Sac.	52	80	154	234	4.5
Jackson, Den.	**68**	**78**	**224**	**302**	**4.4**
McGrady, Tor.	**64**	**105**	**164**	**269**	**4.2**
Taylor, LA-C	71	118	178	296	4.2
Henderson, Cle.	82	71	254	325	4.0
Anstey, Dal.	**41**	**53**	**104**	**157**	**3.8**
Thomas, Phi.	77	107	181	288	3.7
Mercer, Bos.	80	109	171	280	3.5
Cato, Por.	74	91	161	252	3.4
Foyle, G.S.	55	73	111	184	3.3
Knight, Cle.	80	67	186	253	3.2
Closs, LA-C	58	63	105	168	2.9
Anderson, Cle.	66	55	132	187	2.8
Honeycutt, Mil.	38	27	66	93	2.4

FINAL 1997–1998 ROOKIE STATISTICS

FIELD GOAL PCT.	FG	FGA	PCT
Duncan, S.A.	**706**	**1287**	**.549**
Ilgauskas, Cle.	454	876	.518
Funderburke, Sac.	191	390	.490
Henderson, Cle.	348	725	.480
Stewart, Sac.	155	323	.480
Taylor, LA-C	321	675	.476
Fortson, Den.	276	611	.452
Mercer, Bos.	515	1145	.450
McGrady, Tor.	**179**	**398**	**.450**
Thomas, Phi.	306	684	.447

3-PT FIELD GOAL PCT.	3FG	3GA	PCT
Honeycutt, Mil.	29	77	.377
Thomas, Phi.	62	171	.363
Billups, Bos.-Tor.	107	325	.329
Johnson, Sac.	42	128	.328
Washington, Den.	44	137	.321
Van Horn, N.J.	**69**	**224**	**.308**

FINAL 1997–1998 ROOKIE STATISTICS

ASSISTS PER GAME	G	AST	AVG
Knight, Cle.	80	656	8.2
Daniels, Van.	74	334	4.5
Johnson, Sac.	77	329	4.3
Billups, Bos.-Tor.	80	314	3.9
Duncan, S.A.	**82**	**224**	**2.7**
Mercer, Bos.	80	176	2.2
Henderson, Cle.	82	168	2.0
Thomas, Phi.	77	90	1.2
Fortson, Den.	80	76	1.0
Ilgauskas, Cle.	82	71	0.9
Stewart, Sac.	81	61	0.8
Taylor, LA-C	71	53	0.7
Cato, Por.	74	23	0.3

FINAL 1997–1998 ROOKIE STATISTICS

FREE THROW PCT.	FT	FTA	PCT
Anderson, Cle.	275	315	.873
Billups, Bos.-Tor.	226	266	.850
Van Horn, N.J.	**258**	**305**	**.846**
Mercer, Bos.	188	224	.839
Jackson, Den.	**149**	**183**	**.814**
Knight, Cle.	201	251	.801
Washington, Den.	65	83	.783
Fortson, Den.	263	339	.776
Ilgauskas, Cle.	230	302	.762
Thomas, Phi.	171	231	.740

FINAL 1997–1998 ROOKIE STATISTICS

STEALS PER GAME	G	STL	AVG
Knight, Cle.	80	196	2.45
Mercer, Bos.	80	125	1.56
Jackson, Den.	**68**	**105**	**1.54**
Billups, Bos.-Tor.	80	107	1.34
Anderson, Cle.	66	86	1.30
Henderson, Cle.	82	96	1.17
Rhodes, Hou.	58	62	1.07
Van Horn, N.J.	**62**	**64**	**1.03**
Johnson, Sac.	77	64	0.83
Battie, Den.	65	54	0.83

FINAL 1997–1998 ROOKIE STATISTICS

BLOCKS PER GAME	G	BLK	AVG
Duncan, S.A.	**82**	**206**	**2.51**
Stewart, Sac.	81	195	2.41
Ilgauskas, Cle.	82	135	1.65
Closs, LA-C	58	81	1.40
Cato, Por.	74	94	1.27
Battie, Den.	65	69	1.06
McGrady, Tor.	64	61	0.95
Foyle, G.S.	55	52	0.95
Anstey, Dal.	**41**	**27**	**0.66**
Taylor, LA-C	71	40	0.56

FINAL 1997–1998 ROOKIE STATISTICS

MINUTES PER GAME	G	MIN	AVG
Duncan, S.A.	**82**	**3204**	**39.1**
Van Horn, N.J.	**62**	**2325**	**37.5**
Mercer, Bos.	80	2662	33.3
Knight, Cle.	80	2483	31.0
Henderson, Cle.	82	2527	30.8
Jackson, Den.	**68**	**2042**	**30.0**
Johnson, Sac.	77	2266	29.4
Ilgauskas, Cle.	82	2379	29.0
Anderson, Cle.	66	1839	27.9
Billups, Bos.-Tor.	80	2216	27.7

1997–98 ALL-NBA FIRST TEAM

PLAYER, POSITION	TEAM (1st votes)	POINTS
Forward	Karl Malone, Utah (116)	580
Forward	**Tim Duncan, San Antonio (45)**	**370**
Center	Shaquille O'Neal, L.A. Lakers (103)	544
Guard	Michael Jordon, Chicago (116)	580
Guard	Gary Payton, Seattle (108)	561

1997–98 NBA DRAFT: ROUND-BY-ROUND
FIRST ROUND

TEAM	NAME	COLLEGE	HT
1. San Antonio	**Tim Duncan**	**Wake Forest**	**6-11**
2. Philadelphia	**Keith Van Horn**	**Utah**	**6-10**
3. Boston	Chauncey Billups	Colorado	6-3
4. Vancouver	Antonio Daniels	Bowling Green	6-2
5. Denver	Tony Battie	Texas Tech	6-9 1/2
6. Boston (from Dallas)	Ron Mercer	Kentucky	6-7
7. New Jersey	Tim Thomas	Villanova	6-8
8. Golden State	Adonal Foyle	Colgate	6-8 1/2
9. Toronto	**Tracy McGrady**	**Mt. Zion Academy (HS)**	**6-7**
10. Milwaukee	Danny Fortson	Cincinnati	6-7
11. Sacramento	Olivier Saint-Jean	San Jose State	6-5 1/2
12. Indiana	Austin Croshere	Providence	6-9
13. Cleveland	Derek Anderson	Kentucky	6-3 1/2
14. L.A. Clippers	Maurice Taylor	Michigan	6-9
15. Dallas (from Minnesota)	Kelvin Cato	Iowa State	6-10 1/2
16. Cleveland (from Phoenix)	Brevin Knight	Stanford	5-9 1/2

1997–98 NBA DRAFT: ROUND-BY-ROUND
FIRST ROUND (Cont.)

TEAM	NAME	COLLEGE	HT
17. Orlando	Johnny Taylor	Tennessee-Chattanooga	6-7
18. Portland	**Chris Anstey**	**SE Melbourne Magic**	**7-0**
19. Detroit	Scot Pollard	Kansas	6-10
20. Minnesota (from Charlotte via Portland)	Paul Grant	Wisconsin	6-11
21. New Jersey (from L.A. Lakers)	Anthony Parker	Bradley	6-5
22. Atlanta	Ed Gray	California	6-2
23. Seattle	**Bobby Jackson**	**Minnesota**	**5-11**
24. Houston	Rodrick Rhodes	USC	6-6
25. New York	John Thomas	Minnesota	6-7 ½
26. Miami	Charles Smith	New Mexico	6-4 ½
27. Utah	**Jacque Vaughn**	**Kansas**	**5-11**
28. Chicago	Keith Booth	Maryland	6-5

NOTE: There were only 28 selections in the first round. Washington forfeited its pick in the first round.

1997–98 NBA DRAFT: ROUND-BY-ROUND
SECOND ROUND

TEAM	NAME	COLLEGE	HT
30. Houston (from Vancouver)	Serge Zwikker	North Carolina	7-2
31. Miami	Mark Sanford	Washington	6-8 $\frac{1}{2}$
32. Detroit (from San Antonio)	Charles O'Bannon	UCLA	6-5 $\frac{1}{2}$
33. Denver	James Cotton	Long Beach State	6-4
34. Philadelphia	Marko Milic	Smelt Olimpija (Slovenia)	6-6
35. Dallas	Bubba Wells	Austin Peay	6-4
36. Philadelphia (from New Jersey)	Kebu Stewart	Cal State— Bakersfield	6-6
37. Philadelphia (from Toronto)	James Collins	Florida State	6-3
38. Golden State	Marc Jackson	Temple	6-8
39. Milwaukee	Jerald Honeycutt	Tulane	6-7
40. Sacramento	Anthony Johnson	College of Charleston	6-2
41. Seattle (from L.A. Clippers)	Ed Elisma	Georgia Tech	6-8 $\frac{1}{2}$
42. Denver (from Indiana)	Jason Lawson	Villanova	6-9 $\frac{1}{2}$

1997–98 NBA DRAFT: ROUND-BY-ROUND
SECOND ROUND (Cont.)

TEAM	NAME	COLLEGE	HT
43. Phoenix	Stephen Jackson	Butler County (Kansas) CC	6-6
44. Minnesota	Gordon Malone	West Virginia	6-11
45. Cleveland	Cedric Henderson	Memphis	6-6
46. Washington	God Shammgod	Providence	6-0
47. Orlando	Eric Washington	Alabama	6-3
48. Portland	Alvin Williams	Villanova	6-4
49. Washington (from Charlotte)	Predrag Drobnjak	Partizan (Belgrade)	6-10
50. Atlanta (from Detroit)	Alain Digbeu	Villeurbanne (France)	6-5
51. Atlanta	Chris Crawford	Marquette	6-8
52. L.A. Lakers	DeJuan Wheat	Louisville	5-11 $\frac{1}{2}$
53. Vancouver (from Houston)	C.J. Bruton	Indian Hills (Iowa) CC	6-2
54. L.A. Lakers (from New York)	Paul Rogers	Gonzaga	6-11
55. Seattle	Mark Blount	Pittsburgh	6-10

1997–98 NBA DRAFT: ROUND-BY-ROUND
SECOND ROUND (Cont.)

TEAM	NAME	COLLEGE	HT
56. Boston	Ben Pepper	Newcastle Falcons (NBL)	7-0
57. Utah	Nate Erdmann	Oklahoma	6-5
58. Chicago	Roberto Duenas	FC Barcelona (Spain)	7-2

SCHICK NBA ROOKIE OF THE YEAR
(Eddie Gottlieb Trophy)

Selected by Writers and Broadcasters

1952-53 — Don Meineke, Fort Wayne

1953-54 — Ray Felix, Baltimore

1954-55 — Bob Pettit, Milwaukee

1955-56 — Maurice Stokes, Rochester

1956-57 — Tom Heinsohn, Boston

1957-58 — Woody Sauldsberry, Philadelphia

1958-59 — Elgin Baylor, Minneapolis

1959-60 — Wilt Chamberlain, Philadelphia

1960-61 — Oscar Robertson, Cincinnati

1961-62 — Walt Bellamy, Chicago

1962-63 — Terry Dischinger, Chicago

1963-64 — Jerry Lucas, Cincinnati

1964-65 — Willis Reed, New York

1965-66 — Rick Barry, San Francisco

1966-67 — Dave Bing, Detroit

1967-68 — Earl Monroe, Baltimore

1968-69 — Wes Unseld, Baltimore

1969-70 — Kareem Abdul-Jabbar, Milwaukee

SCHICK NBA ROOKIE OF THE YEAR (Cont.)
(Eddie Gottlieb Trophy)

1970-71	—	Dave Cowens, Boston
		Geoff Petrie, Portland
1971-72	—	Sidney Wicks, Portland
1972-73	—	Bob McAdoo, Buffalo
1973-74	—	Ernie DiGregorio, Buffalo
1974-75	—	Keith Wilkes, Golden State
1975-76	—	Alvan Adams, Phoenix
1976-77	—	Adrian Dantley, Buffalo
1977-78	—	Walter Davis, Phoenix
1978-79	—	Phil Ford, Kansas City
1979-80	—	Larry Bird, Boston
1980-81	—	Darrell Griffith, Utah
1981-82	—	Buck Williams, New Jersey
1982-83	—	Terry Cummings, San Diego
1983-84	—	Ralph Sampson, Houston
1984-85	—	Michael Jordan, Chicago
1985-86	—	Patrick Ewing, New York
1986-87	—	Chuck Person, Indiana
1987-88	—	Mark Jackson, New York

SCHICK NBA ROOKIE OF THE YEAR (Cont.)
(Eddie Gottlieb Trophy)

1988-89 — Mitch Richmond, Golden State

1989-90 — David Robinson, San Antonio

1990-91 — Derrick Coleman, New Jersey

1991-92 — Larry Johnson, Charlotte

1992-93 — Shaquille O'Neal, Orlando

1993-94 — Chris Webber, Golden State

1994-95 — Grant Hill, Detroit

Jason Kidd, Dallas

1995-96 — Damon Stoudamire, Toronto

1996-97 — Allen Iverson, Philadelphia

1997-98 — Tim Duncan, San Antonio

ALL-TIME ALL-ROOKIE TEAMS

Selected by NBA coaches

1962-63

Terry Dischinger, Chicago

Chet Walker, Syracuse

Zelmo Beaty, St. Louis

John Havlicek, Boston

Dave DeBusschere, Detroit

1963-64

Jerry Lucas, Cincinnati

Gus Johnson, Baltimore

Nate Thurmond, San Francisco

Art Heyman, New York

Rod Thorn, Baltimore

1964-65

Willis Reed, New York

Jim Barnes, New York

Howard Komives, New York

Lucious Jackson, Philadelphia

Wally Jones, Baltimore

Joe Caldwell, Detroit

ALL-ROOKIE TEAMS (Cont.)

Selected by NBA coaches

1965-66
Rick Barry, San Francisco
Billy Cunningham, Philadelphia
Tom Van Arsdale, Detroit
Dick Van Arsdale, New York
Fred Hetzel, San Francisco

1966-67
Lou Hudson, St. Louis
Jack Marin, Baltimore
Erwin Mueller, Chicago
Cazzie Russell, New York
Dave Bing, Detroit

1967-68
Earl Monroe, Baltimore
Bob Rule, Seattle
Walt Frazier, New York
Al Tucker, Seattle
Phil Jackson, New York

ALL-ROOKIE TEAMS (Cont.)

Selected by NBA coaches

1968-69

Wes Unseld, Baltimore

Elvin Hayes, San Diego

Bill Hewitt, Los Angeles

Art Harris, Seattle

Gary Gregor, Phoenix

1969-70

Kareem Abdul-Jabbar, Milwaukee

Bob Dandridge, Milwaukee

Jo Jo White, Boston

Mike Davis, Baltimore

Dick Garrett, Los Angeles

1970-71

Geoff Petrie, Portland

Dave Cowens, Boston

Pete Maravich, Atlanta

Calvin Murphy, San Diego

Bob Lanier, Detroit

ALL-ROOKIE TEAMS (Cont.)

Selected by NBA coaches

1971-72
Elmore Smith, Buffalo
Sidney Wicks, Portland
Austin Carr, Cleveland
Phil Chenier, Baltimore
Clifford Ray, Chicago

1972-73
Bob McAdoo, Buffalo
Lloyd Neal, Portland
Fred Boyd, Philadelphia
Dwight Davis, Cleveland
Jim Price, Los Angeles

1973-74
Ernie DiGregorio, Buffalo
Ron Behagen, Kansas City/Omaha
Mike Bantom, Phoenix
John Brown, Atlanta
Nick Weatherspoon, Capital

ALL-ROOKIE TEAMS (Cont.)

Selected by NBA coaches

1974-75

Keith Wilkes, Golden State
John Drew, Atlanta
Scott Wedman, Kansas City/Omaha
Tom Burleson, Seattle
Brian Winters, Los Angeles

1975-76

Alvan Adams, Phoenix
Gus Williams, Golden State
Joe Meriweather, Houston
John Shumate, Phoenix-Buffalo
Lionel Hollins, Portland

1976-77

Adrian Dantley, Buffalo
Scott May, chicago
Mitch Kupchak, Washington
John Lucas, Houston
Ron Lee, Phoenix

ALL-ROOKIE TEAMS (Cont.)

Selected by NBA coaches

1977-78
Walter Davis, Phoenix
Marques Johnson, Milwaukee
Bernard King, New Jersey
Jack Sikma, Seattle
Norm Nixon, Los Angeles

1978-79
Phil Ford, Kansas City
Mychal Thompson, Portland
Ron Brewer, Portland
Reggie Theus, Chicago
Terry Tyler, Detroit

1979-80
Larry Bird, Boston
Magic Johnson, Los Angeles
Bill Cartwright, New York
Calvin Natt, New Jersey-Portland
David Greenwood, Chicago

ALL-ROOKIE TEAMS (Cont.)

Selected by NBA coaches

1980-81
Joe Barry Carroll, Golden State
Darrell Griffith, Utah
Larry Smith, Golden State
Kevin McHale, Boston
Kelvin Ramsey, Portland

1981-82
Kelly Tripucka, Detroit
Jay Vincent, Dallas
Isiah Thomas, Detroit
Buck Williams, New Jersey
Jeff Ruland, Washington

1982-83
Terry Cummings, San Diego
Clark Kellogg, Indiana
Dominique Wilkins, Atlanta
James Worthy, Los Angeles
Quintin Dailey, Chicago

ALL-ROOKIE TEAMS (Cont.)

Selected by NBA coaches

1983-84

Ralph Sampson, Houston
Steve Stipanovich, Indiana
Byron Scott, Los Angeles
Jeff Malone, Washington
Thurl Bailey, Utah
Darrell Walker, New York

1984-85

Michael Jordan, Chicago
Hakeem Olajuwon, Houston
Sam Bowie, Portland
Charles Barkley, Philadelphia
Sam Perkins, Dallas

1985-86

Xavier McDaniel, Seattle
Patrick Ewing, New York
Karl Malone, Utah
Joe Dumars, Detroit
Charles Oakley, Chicago

ALL-ROOKIE TEAMS (Cont.)

Selected by NBA coaches

1986-87
Brad Daugherty, Cleveland
Ron Harper, Cleveland
Chuck Person, Indiana
Roy Tarpley, Dallas
John Williams, Cleveland

1987-88
Mark Jackson, New York
Armon Gilliam, Phoenix
Kenny Smith, Sacramento
Greg Anderson, San Antonio
Derrick McKey, Seattle

1988-89
First
Mitch Richmond, Golden State
Willie Anderson, San Antonio
Hersey Hawkins, Philadelphia
Rik Smits, Indiana
Charles Smith, L.A. Clippers

ALL-ROOKIE TEAMS (Cont.)

Selected by NBA coaches

1988-89
Second
Brian Shaw, Boston
Rex Chapman, Charlotte
Chris Morris, New Jersey
Rod Strickland, New York
Kevin Edwards, Miami

1989-90
First
David Robinson, San Antonio
Tim Hardaway, Golden State
Vlade Divac, L.A. Lakers
Sherman Douglas, Miami
Poon Richardson, Minnesota
Second
J.R. Reid, Charlotte
Sean Elliott, San Antonio
Stacey King, Chicago
Blue Edwards, Utah
Glen Rice, Miami

ALL-ROOKIE TEAMS (Cont.)

Selected by NBA coaches

1990-91
First
Kendall Gill, Charlotte

Dennis Scott, Orlando

Dee Brown, Boston

Lionel Simmons, Sacramento

Derrick Coleman, New Jersey
Second
Chris Jackson, Denver

Gary Payton, Seattle

Felton Spencer, Minnesota

Travis Mays, Sacramento

Willie Burton, Miami

1991-92
First
Larry Johnson, Charlotte

Dikembe Mutombo, Denver

Billy Owens, Golden State

Steve Smith, Miami

Stacey Augmon, Atlanta

ALL-ROOKIE TEAMS (Cont.)

Selected by NBA coaches

1991-92
Second
Rick Fox Boston
Terrell Brandon, Cleveland
Larry Stewart, Washington
Stanley Roberts, Orlando
Mark Macon, Denver

1992-93
First
Shaquille O'Neal, Orlando
Alonzo Mourning, Charlotte
Christian Laettner, Minnesota
Tom Gugliotta, Washington
LaPhonso Ellis, Denver
Second
Walt Williams, Sacramento
Robert Horry, Houston
Latrell Sprewell, Golden State
Clarence Weatherspoon, Philadelphia
Richard Dumas, Phoenix

ALL-ROOKIE TEAMS (Cont.)

Selected by NBA coaches

1993-94
First
Chris Webber, Golden State
Anfernee Hardaway, Orlando
Vin Baker, Milwaukee
Jamal Mashburn, Dallas
Isaiah Rider, Minnesota
Second
Dino Radja, Boston
Nick Van Exel, L.A. Lakers
Shawn Bradley, Philadelphia
Toni Kukoo, Chicago
Lindsey Hunter, Detroit

1994-95
First
Jason Kidd, Dallas
Grant Hill, Detroit
Glenn Robinson, Milwaukee
Eddie Jones, L.A. Lakers
Brian Grant, Sacramento

ALL-ROOKIE TEAMS (Cont.)

Selected by NBA coaches

1994-95
Second
Juwan Howard, Washington

Eric Montross, Boston

Wesley Person, Phoenix

Jalen Rose, Denver

Donyell Marshall, Minnesota-Golden State

Sharone Wright, Philadelphia

1995-96
First
Damon Stoudamire, Toronto

Joe Smith, Golden State

Jerry Stackhouse, Philadelphia

Antonio McDyess, Denver

Arvydas Sabonis, Portland

Michael Finley, Phoenix

ALL-ROOKIE TEAMS (Cont.)

Selected by NBA coaches

1995-96
Second
Kevin Garnett, Minnesota

Bryant Reeves, Vancouver

Brent Barry, L.A. Clippers

Rasheed Wallace, Washington

Tyus Edney, Sacramento

1996-97
First
Shareef Abdur-Rahim, Vancouver

Allen Iverson, Philadelphia

Stephon Marbury, Minnesota

Marcus Camby, Toronto

Antoine Walker, Boston
Second
Kerry Kittles, New Jersey

Ray Allen, Milwaukee

Travis Knight, L.A. Lakers

Kobe Bryant, L.A. Lakers

Matt Maloney, Houston

ALL-ROOKIE TEAMS (Cont.)

Selected by NBA coaches

1997-98
First
Tim Duncan, San Antonio
Keith Van Horn, New Jersey
Brevin Knight, Cleveland
Zydrunas Ilgauskas, Cleveland
Ron Mercer, Boston
Second
Tim Thomas, Philadelphia
Cedric Henderson, Cleveland
Derek Anderson, Cleveland
Maurice Taylor, L.A. Clippers
Bobby Jackson, Denver

ALL-TIME ROOKIES IN NBA ALL-STAR GAMES
(* = starters)

ROOKIE	TEAM	YEAR
Paul Arizin	Philadelphia	1951
*Bob Cousy	Boston	1951
Larry Foust	Fort Wayne	1951
*Ray Felix	Baltimore	1954
Don Sunderlage	Milwaukee	1954
Bob Pettit	Milwaukee	1955
Frank Selvy	Milwaukee	1955
Maurice Stokes	Rochester	1956
*Tom Heinsohn	Boston	1957
Elgin Baylor	Minneapolis	1959 All-Star Co-MVP
*Wilt Chamberlain	Philadelphia	1960 All-Star MVP
*Oscar Robertson	Cincinnati	1961 All-Star MVP
Jerry West	L.A. Lakers	1961
*Walt Bellamy	Chicago	1962
Terry Dischinger	Chicago	1963
*Jerry Lucas	Cincinnati	1964
*Luke Jackson	Philadelphia	1965
Willis Reed	New York	1965
*Rick Barry	San Francisco	1966

ALL-TIME ROOKIES IN NBA ALL-STAR GAMES
(Cont.)

(* = starters)

ROOKIE	TEAM	YEAR
*Elvin Hayes	San Diego	1969
Wes Unseld	Baltimore	1969
Kareem Abdul-Jabbar	Milwaukee	1970
John Johnson	Cleveland	1971
Geoff Petrie	Portland	1971
Sidney Wicks	Portland	1972
Alvan Adams	Phoenix	1976
Walter Davis	Phoenix	1978
Larry Bird	Boston	1980
Bill Cartwright	New York	1980
*Magic Johnson	L.A. Lakers	1980
*Isiah Thomas	Detroit	1982
Kelly Tripucka	Detroit	1982
Buck Williams	New Jersey	1982
Ralph Sampson	Houston	1984
*Michael Jordan	Chicago	1985
Hakeem Olajuwon	Houston	1985
Patrick Ewing	New York	1986

ALL-TIME ROOKIES IN NBA ALL-STAR GAMES
(Cont.)
(* = starters)

Dikembe Mutombo	Denver	1992
*Shaquille OíNeal	Orlando	1993
*Grant Hill	Detroit	1995
Tim Duncan	**San Antonio**	**1998**

ALL-TIME ROOKIE
ALL-NBA FIRST TEAM SELECTIONS

PLAYER	SEASON	TEAM
Tim Duncan	**1997-98**	**San Antonio Spurs**
Larry Bird	1979-80	Boston Celtics
Wes Unseld	1968-69	Baltimore Bullets
Rick Barry	1965-66	San Francisco Warriors
Oscar Robertson	1960-61	Cincinnati Royals
Wilt Chamberlain	1959-60	Philadelphia Warriors
Elgin Baylor	1958-59	Minneapolis Lakers
Bob Pettit	1954-55	Milwaukee Hawks
Alex Groza	1949-50	Indianapolis Olympians

NOTE: Players selected to the All-NBA First Team for the 1946-47 season, the league's inaugural campaign, are not included on this list.

ALL-TIME ROOKIE NBA PLAYER OF THE WEEK/MONTH WINNERS

19 rookies have won NBA Player of the Week honors 25 times and NBA Player of the Month honors once since the awards began to be given out in the 1979-80 season:

PLAYER OF THE WEEK

Pos.	Player	Team	Week Ending
C	**Tim Duncan**	**San Antonio Spurs**	**03/01/98**
G	Allen Iverson	Philadelphia 76ers	04/13/97
C	Arvydas Sabonis	Portland Trail Blazers	03/31/96
G	Jason Kidd	Dallas Mavericks	03/19/95
F/C	Chris Webber	Golden State Warriors	01/19/94
C	Shaquille O'Neal	Orlando Magic	11/15/92
C	Alonzo Mourning	Charlotte Hornets	04/18/93
F	Larry Johnson	Charlotte Hornets	03/22/92
G/F	Dennis Scott	Orlando Magic	03/10/91
F	Lionel Simmons	Sacramento Kings	02/17/91
C	David Robinson	San Antonio Spurs	04/22/90
C	David Robinson	San Antonio Spurs	03/25/90
C	David Robinson	San Antonio Spurs	02/25/90
G	Tim Hardaway	Golden State Warriors	02/04/90

ALL-TIME ROOKIE NBA PLAYER OF THE WEEK/MONTH WINNERS
(Cont.)

F	Charles Barkley	Philadelphia 76ers	03/30/86
F	Charles Barkley	Philadelphia 76ers	03/02/86
F	Charles Barkley	Philadelphia 76ers	02/26/86
C	Patrick Ewing	New York Knicks	11/17/85
G	Michael Jordan	Chicago Bulls	01/20/85
F	Kelly Tripucka	Detroit Pistons	03/14/82
F	Jay Vincent	Dallas Mavericks	02/14/82
G	Magic Johnson	Los Angeles Lakers	03/16/80
F	Larry Bird	Boston Celtics	03/02/80
G	Magic Johnson	Los Angeles Lakers	03/16/80
G	Magic Johnson	Los Angeles Lakers	11/11/79

PLAYER OF THE MONTH

Pos.	Player	Team	Month
F	Larry Bird	Boston Celtics	Feb., 1980

About the Author

Mike Monroe has covered the Denver Nuggets and the NBA for the *Denver Post* since 1985. A sports journalist for 30 years, Monroe was the President of the Professional Basketball Writers Association in 1996 and 1997. He was also the 1997 Colorado Sports Writer of the Year.

Monroe graduated from the University of Colorado in 1971. He is a native of Collinsville, Ill., and still brags that the Collinsville Kahoks have won more games than any high school team in the nation. Monroe gave up playing basketball when he turned 50 in 1997, but he still skis well and plays golf badly.